BROKEN
SPIRITS

BROKEN SPIRITS

The Treatment of Traumatized Asylum Seekers, Refugees, War and Torture Victims

edited by
John P. Wilson, Ph.D. • Boris Drožđek, M.D., M.A.

Brunner-Routledge
New York • Hove

Published in 2004 by
Brunner-Routledge
270 Madison Avenue
New York, NY 10016
www.brunner-routledge.com

Published in Great Britain by
Brunner-Routledge
27 Church Road
Hove
East Sussex BN3 2FA U.K.
www.brunner-routledge.co.uk

Brunner-Routledge is an imprint of the Taylor & Francis Group.
Printed in the United States of America on acid-free paper.

10 9 8 7 6 5 4 3 2 1

Library of Congress Cataloging-in-Publication Data

Broken spirits : the treatment of traumatized asylum seekers, refugees, war and
torture victims / John P. Wilson, Boris Drožđek, editors.
     p. ; cm.
     Includes bibliographical references and index.
     ISBN 0-415-94397-3 (hardcover : alk. paper)
     1. Post-traumatic stress disorder—Treatment. 2. Refugees—Rehabilitation. 3.
War victims—Rehabilitation. 4. Torture victims—Rehabilitation. 5. Refugees—Mental health services. 6. War victims—Mental health services. 7. Torture
victims—Mental health services. 8. War—Psychological aspects. 9. Psychiatry,
Transcultural.
     [DNLM: 1. Stress Disorders, Post-Traumatic—therapy. 2. Human Rights
Abuses—psychology. 3. Refugees—psychology. 4. Stress, Psychological—
psychology. 5. Survivors—psychology. 6. Torture—psychology. WM 170 B867
2004] I. Wilson, John P. (John Preston) II. Drožđek, Boris. III. Title.

RC552.P67B76 2004
616.85'21—dc22

                                                                    2003027251

Contents

Foreword

This is a challenging and important book. Its contributors build a comprehensive and compelling picture of the impact of the complex emergencies of war, torture, refugee status, asylum seeking, and internal displacement on the health and well-being of the many populations so affected, and indeed all those who would offer their care. It includes many distinguished contributors to the fields of refugee mental health, trauma, and grief and builds on the work of other pioneers such as Richard Mollica.

This is a confronting book. To know of the suffering, to hear again and again of the horror, and to read of the attempts to make meaning of it and to help those affected to heal mean we must acknowledge this vast human experience. It is painful to do so.

This book is important because it is a handbook by which we can, bit by bit, confront and learn about the impacts of dislocation, trauma, and loss; of political persecution and human malevolence; and social systems involving abuse, neglect, and ethnic and cultural rejection. We can learn about what we might do, both to assist and as advocates to address these impacts and their mental health consequences. We can learn again the lessons so easily "forgotten" about what we can do for traumatized asylum seekers, refugees, and war and torture victims. This book is a handbook, well informed by the learned knowledge, the empirical research, the clinical and social experience, and the wisdom of the contributors. It provides knowledge and tools to be taken up to address these mental health impacts, and interventions that can work "across the ethno–cultural divide."

Many of the issues presented are known intellectually, but not known. The nature and forms of torture, for instance, can be listed, but doubted when described by an unwelcomed asylum seeker. This intellectual splitting is described well, showing how easily it can apply to those who would help and to their societies.

The historical and socio-cultural perspectives that influence recep-
tiveness to these populations and their needs are well highlighted, and
can inform policy makers as well as clinicians. They are a global challenge. Indeed the response of democratic nations, described by many in
this book, as increasingly repressive and rejecting can damage the inherent democratic strengths of these institutions, even shifting them to take
up some of the characteristics of the nations from which the refugees
who seek their acceptance have fled.

In addition to the impacts from the multiple smaller wars and complex emergencies in developing nations, the public health challenges of
these traumatizations across the populations of refugees, and those
internally displaced, of up to 40 million people worldwide constitute
severe threats to human and social, cultural, and community development worldwide. The strategies described by the various contributors
provide frameworks for mental health interventions, which it is noted
must at times be pragmatic in addressing what can be achieved, consultative, and as advocacy.

Theoretical structures for understanding and response are described
by a number of the contributors. These are frequently complex, reflecting the complexities of this field. Many will be validated by either
empirical studies or by their inherent utility and perceived benefits. It
must be remembered that they also serve the valuable functions of providing structure in the face of chaos, enabling workers in health and
welfare systems to respond to what may seem otherwise overwhelming
and insurmountable. Writers provide guidance to these issues, both in
social, political, and ethical frameworks, as well as clinical. They also
take account of the special transference and counter-transference
themes to be dealt with when engaging in therapy with those who have
had such horrific experiences, and the needs for systems of support and
supervision.

The knowledge and techniques presented in this volume cover the
full range of issues that need to be understood and dealt with, including
addressing the needs of children, adolescents and families, women and
men, and peoples of many cultures, ethnicities, and languages; from
assessment, diagnoses, and cultural idioms of distress to psychothera-
pies, non-verbal and experiential therapies; from physical health care to
psychopharmacotherapy. We learn of inequities, diversities, and complexities and about speaking or not speaking about what has happened
to us. We learn to consider the trauma archetype. The needs for safety,
security, and belief in survival to build trust in the world and a sense of
worth are seen as critical. Research described shows the possibility of
very good outcomes over time when environments are positive and
secure, and the risks of increasing vulnerability and pathology when
they are not. Sometimes stories can only be told when there is safety,
the possibility of a future, when one is drawn back from the "abyss";
when the shame, guilt, and anger can be faced in circumstance of trust;
when "perennial" losses can be accommodated; when needs for human

rights and justice can be expressed; when therapists and others can bear to hear; and when compassion abides.

Each and every one of the many contributors describes a "new" facet, aspect, or component of this vast and terrible field. We have yet to understand and to develop social, political, and human systems that negate the human malevolence that can lead to such outcomes; prevent its powerful emergence and actions; and that can assist us to understand and deal with this aspect of ourselves and others in all human societies. This volume helps us understand some of these impacts and highlights how important such prevention will be, because neither as mental health professionals nor even as social engineers can we adequately undo the consequences.

Much further research is clearly needed to address these issues, and, as highlighted by many contributors, so are new methodologies to meet the ethical, humanitarian, and scientific requirements of understanding the needs of, and outcomes for, such vulnerable populations. Balancing traditional science, epidemiological studies, and clinical trials with inherent wisdom, clinical intuition, and innovation is difficult — but a very appropriate requirement if compassionate, effective, and efficient responses are to be developed to meet this public health challenge.

We learn of the spirit, and the spirits of all involved; of fighting spirits; of healing spirits; of good and bad spirits; and sadly of broken spirits. Yet even these may be helped to be "transcendent." This is a good book — one we may hesitate to read, yet one we will never forget.

In conclusion, this work speaks of horror, of the profound consequences of the darkest and most deadly of human experience. Yet it gives pathways and understandings for response. Its contributions speak with, and of, soul, suffering, and strength. Most importantly, it is ultimately hopeful and compassionate, balancing the "dark side" with forces for good.

Professor Beverly Raphael
Director, Centre for Mental Health
North Sydney
New South Wales

About the Editors

John P. Wilson, Ph.D., is a professor of psychology at Cleveland State University in Cleveland, Ohio, USA, and a Fulbright Scholar. He is cofounder of the International Society for Traumatic Stress Studies, a fellow of the American Institute of Stress and diplomate and fellow of the American Academy of Experts in Traumatic Stress, and a board certified expert in forensic traumatology. He is the author of over 12 books, 30 monographs, and numerous articles on traumatic stress.

Boris Drožđek, M.D., M.A., is psychiatrist at the Outpatient and Day Treatment Centre for Asylum Seekers and Refugees/GGz's-Hertogenbosch, the Netherlands. He specializes in treatment of asylum seekers and refugees/torture survivors, and initiated development of a treatment services network. He is also a teacher in social psychiatry, and international director of the Summer School of Psychotrauma in Dubrovnik, Croatia. He publishes in the field of psycho-traumatology, and teaches and gives training and workshops for different agencies on a regular basis in the Netherlands and abroad. He also works for different NGOs in post-war areas.

Contributors

Hubertus Adam, M.D., is a child and adolescent psychiatrist and psychotherapist, psychoanalytic couple and family therapist, and head of the Outpatient Department for Refugee Children and Their Families at the Clinic of Child and Adolescent Psychiatry at the University Clinics of Hamburg. He is also medical director of Stefanie Graf's foundation, "Children for Tomorrow," with psychotherapeutic projects for war-traumatized children in Kosovo, South Africa, Mozambique, and Hamburg.

Libby Tata Arcel is an associate professor of clinical psychology and a psychotherapist affiliated with the Institute of Psychology, University of Copenhagen, Denmark. She has been a senior consultant for the European Union, Human Rights and Democratization Section (1993–1995), and a consultant for the International Criminal Tribunal for former Yugoslavia (ICTY), Victims and Witness Support Section (1994–1998). Also, she worked as a senior health consultant for the International Rehabilitation Council for Torture Victims (IRCT; 1993–2001), and a research coordinator at the Center for Torture Victims, Most, Sarajevo (1998–2003).

Jorge Aroche is a clinical psychologist and executive director of the New South Wales, Australia Service for the Treatment and Rehabilitation of Torture and Trauma Survivors, better known as STARTTS. He is an executive member of the Forum of Australian Services for Survivors of Torture and Trauma (FASSTT), the elected representative of the Asia-Pacific region of the International Society for Health and Human Rights, and has presented widely on clinical and settlement issues for traumatized refugees in national and international conferences. He has co-authored a number of articles as part of STARTTS' growing research program.

Julia Bala, Ph.D., is a psychologist and systems-oriented psychotherapist, working for Foundation Centrum 45, Treatment of and Research into the Consequences of Organized Violence, De Vonk Amsterdam, and associated with Pharos, Knowledge Centre for Refugees and Health, Utrecht. She has been working with refugee children and families in the Netherlands since 1993 and is author of many articles in professional journals, and contributor to several books and research publications.

Bijou Blick, M.D., has worked in Sydney as a community pediatric medical officer since 1988. She has a strong interest in health education and health promotion programs for the community. She also has research interests in the systemic review of child health practice and the use of information systems in community pediatrics. Her work regularly involves assessing children and their families as part of a multidisciplinary community pediatric team. She has academic qualifications in community pediatrics, public health, child mental health, and child development.

Hanneke Bot is a sociologist and Dutch registered psychotherapist. She works in the unit Phoenix for the treatment of asylum seekers and refugees with psychiatric problems, part of a large psychiatric hospital, De Gelderse Roos in Wolfheze. She is currently working on her Ph.D. in "interpreting in mental health" at the University of Utrecht, the Netherlands.

Mariano J. Coello is a clinical psychologist who has worked for the last seventeen years with migrants and refugees, survivors of torture, and organized violence. Since 1991, Mariano has held several clinical positions at the New South Wales Service, Australia for the Treatment and Rehabilitation of Torture and Trauma Survivors (STARTTS), where he is currently the clinical services and research coordinator. He is responsible for the quality and supervision of STARTTS' clinical services which are provided across the state. He has conducted and participated in several successful projects on psychosocial and mental health issues affecting children and young refugee survivors of war-organized violence and has represented STARTTS on a number of forums and conferences, nationally and internationally, on issues related to refugees in general, and torture and trauma survivors specifically.

Joop de Jong, M.D., Ph.D., is professor of mental health and culture at the Vrije Universiteit in Amsterdam. He is the director of TPO (Transcultural Psychosocial Organization), Peace of Mind, a WHO Collaborating Center for Refugees and Ethnic Minorities. TPO has developed or supported psychosocial and mental health programs in seventeen countries in Africa, Asia, Europe, and Latin America. In the Netherlands, TPO is carrying out several epidemiological studies on immigrants and refugees. Joop de Jong publishes in the field of cultural psychiatry and psychotherapy, epidemiology, and public mental health. In addition, he works part-time as a psychiatrist/psychotherapist. In the past, he worked for seven years as a tropical doctor, public health officer, and psychiatrist/psychotherapist in Africa and Asia.

Bram de Winter is a trained teacher in physical education. He started his career in the Prof. W.P.J. Pompe Clinic in Nijmegen, the Netherlands as a psychomotor therapist for psychologically disturbed criminals. He studied andragology, the change processes in adults, at the University of Nijmegen and did the basic training in psychotherapy. For twenty-three years, he was a teacher of a postacademic course for psychomotor therapy, and he has worked for more than 25 years in a psychiatric setting. Since 1997, he has been affiliated with the Day Treatment Centre for Asylum Seekers and Refugees/GGz's-Hertogenbosch, the Netherlands.

Letty Doorschodt has been a music therapist since 1987. She has practiced in several psychiatric clinics in the Netherlands, and has worked for three years with traumatized refugees within the Day Treatment Centre for Asylum Seekers and Refugees/GGz's-Hertogenbosch. She has also worked as a volunteer within the Psychiatric Outreach Program of the Isoka District Hospital, Zambia.

Michael Dudley, M.D., is a child and adolescent psychiatrist at Sydney Children's Hospital and Prince of Wales Hospitals, and is senior lecturer in psychiatry at the University of New South Wales. He chairs Suicide Prevention Australia (SPA), a peak organization with a history of networking, training, and advocacy for suicide prevention and has published in the field of suicide research and prevention, where he has undertaken epidemiological and service-oriented studies. He has had a long-term interest in psychiatry, contemporary culture, spirituality, and human rights, and has written on the image of psychiatry in contemporary Australian fiction, psychiatry under the Nazis, the relationship of psychiatry and religion, and self-harm among asylum seekers in immigration detention centers.

Solvig Ekblad, Ph.D., is a licensed clinical psychologist, and associate professor in transcultural psychology at the Karolinska Institutet (adjunct at the Division of Psychiatry, Neurotec Department), Stockholm, Sweden; head of Unit for Immigrant Environment and Health, at the National Institute of Psychosocial Factors and Health, Stockholm. She is in charge of the research program Migration and Health, which studies psychosocial factors to promote, or counteract, the successful integration of immigrants and refugees in a host society. She has research grants from the National Swedish Integration Office, European Refugee Fund, Swedish Council for Social Research, and Stockholm County Council. Internationally, she has been consultant to several U.N. agencies and co-chaired, together with Prof. Derrick Silov (Australia, foreign adjunct professor at the Karolinska Institutet), the International Committee on Refugees and Other Migrants, World Federation for Mental Health (1997–2002). She has written many articles and book chapters and has presented papers on international and national conferences in the field of migration and mental health.

Carla Ferstman is the legal director of the Redress Trust, a human rights organization that assists torture survivors seeking justice and reparation. She is a member of the UK Foreign and Commonwealth Office Expert Panel on Torture and an associate member of the Council of the International Criminal Bar. Ms. Ferstman has wide experience in legal reform and capacity building in postconflict situations and in 1999 was appointed Executive Legal Advisor of Bosnia and Herzegovina's Commission for Real Property Claims of Displaced Persons and Refugees (CRPC). She has an LL.B. from the University of British Columbia and an LL.M. from New York University.

Matthew J. Friedman, M.D., Ph.D., is executive director of the National Center for Post-Traumatic Stress Disorder (PTSD), headquartered at the Veteran's Administration Medical Center in White River Junction, Vermont; and professor of psychiatry and pharmacology at Dartmouth Medical School, Hanover, New Hampshire. He has worked with PTSD patients as a clinician and researcher for twenty years and has published extensively on stress and PTSD. Dr. Friedman is past president of the International Society for Traumatic Stress Studies and has recently published books on the neurobiological basis of stress, evidence-based treatment guidelines for PTSD, and ethnocultural aspects of PTSD.

Rudolf Gregurek, M.D., is an assistant professor at the School of Medicine, University of Zagreb, Zagreb, Croatia and head of Clinic for Psychological Medicine, University Hospital, Zagreb. He teaches psychiatry, liaison psychiatry, and psychological medicine. His research focuses on psychotherapeutic work with traumatized patients and on caregiving for refugees.

Ton Haans is a clinical psychologist/psychotherapist. From 1976 to 2003 he was attached to Centrum '45, the Dutch national agency for assistance to survivors of political violence. Along with his therapeutic work he was coordinator of the training department. He is registered supervisor of the Dutch Group Psychotherapeutic Society and runs a private consultation and supervision practice.

Jane Herlihy, M.D., is a clinical psychologist working with traumatized refugees and asylum seekers in London. Her research interests are in the contributions that psychological understanding can offer to the process of decision making in asylum law.

Johannes E. Hovens is a psychiatrist, clinical psychologist, and psychotherapist. He has published extensively on posttraumatic stress disorder. Currently he is head of the teaching department of DeltaBouman Psychiatric Teaching Hospital at Poortugaal, the Netherlands.

James M. Jaranson, M.D., M.A., M.P.H., is co-chair of the World Psychiatric Association (WPA) Section on Psychological Consequences of Torture and Persecution, the U.S. representative at the International Rehabilitation Council for Torture Victims, WPA independent expert, and member of the Executive Committee. He is also the principal investigator of the NIMH-funded epidemiology project surveying torture and violence in Somali and Ethiopian refugees in Minnesota, with faculty appointments in the Department of Psychiatry and the Division of Epidemiology, University of Minnesota (1998–2003). He is the first psychiatrist and has been medical director of the Center for Victims of Torture, Minneapolis since 2001.

Marianne Juhler, M.D., DMSc., is associate professor of neurosurgery at Rigshospitalet (Copenhagen University Hospital), and has been a consultant at the Rehabilitation Centre for Torture Victims (RCT), Copenhagen since its inception in 1993. She is author and co-author of textbooks in neurology and neurosurgery as well as international publications on basic neuroscience and clinical neuroscience.

Sylvia Karcher is a psychotherapist and physical therapist for concentrative movement therapy. She works in various clinics, in freelance practice, and in continuing training in concentrative movement therapy. She has worked as a therapist at the Berlin Center for the Treatment of Torture Victims from 1992 until her retirement in October 2003.

Marianne C. Kastrup, M.D., Ph.D., is the head of the Centre for Transcultural Psychiatry, Department of Psychiatry, Rigshospitalet, Copenhagen, Denmark. She is also the WPA (World Psychiatric Association) Zonal Representative for Northern Europe, secretary general of the European Association of Psychiatrists, member of the Expert Advisory Board for Mental Health within the World Health Organization (WHO), and member and former chair of the WPA Standing Committee for the Review of Abuse of Psychiatry.

J. David Kinzie, M.D., is professor of psychiatry and director of the Torture Treatment Center of Oregon and the Child Traumatic Stress Center of Oregon, located at the Oregon Health and Sciences University, Portland. He founded the Intercultural Psychiatric Program in 1977 and personally has a caseload of Cambodian, Somalian, and Central American patients. He is a distinguished life fellow of the American Psychiatric Association.

Johan Lansen, M.D., is a psychiatrist, psychoanalyst, and group psycho-therapist. He is the emeritus director of the Jewish Sinai Center in the Netherlands, the center for treatment of victims of the Nazi Holocaust and their children. He has been treating traumatized refugees for many years and is trainer and supervisor to centers treating refugees in Europe. He is a member of the Scientific Advisory Council of the War Trauma Foundation in the Netherlands, focusing on training profession-als in areas hit by organized man-made violence. He is involved in research on the emotional impact of trauma therapy on therapists and has developed a particular model for supervision in this field.

Sarah Mares, M.D., is a child and family psychiatrist with particular clinical interests in the prevention of child abuse and neglect, and inter-vention in infancy and early childhood. She has undertaken multiple assessments and follow-ups of children and families in immigration detention centers over the last two years and is an active advocate for change of Australia's current immigration policy. She is an experienced postgraduate educator, currently director of the NSW Institute of Psy-chiatry's Clinical Teaching Unit, and an active member of the local Medical Board program for impaired doctors.

Alexander C. McFarlane, M.D., is head of the Department of Psychia-try at the University of Adelaide and a past president of the Interna-tional Society for Traumatic Stress Studies. He has worked with disaster and war-affected communities in Asia, the Middle East, and Europe as well as refugees coming to Australia. His research covers a range of areas including epidemiology and neuroimaging.

Jens Modvig, M.D., Ph.D., specialized in epidemiology. He has been engaged in public health and social medicine at the University of Copenhagen, Denmark and City of Copenhagen until he assumed the position of medical director in the International Rehabilitation Council for Torture Victims (IRCT) in 1999. From 2000–2003, he served as sec-retary general for the IRCT, which in 2003 received the Hilton Humani-tarian Prize.

Louise Newman, M.D., is a child and adolescent psychiatrist with a par-ticular interest in childhood trauma and developmental neurobiology. She is the chair of the Faculty of Child and Adolescent Psychiatry of the Royal Australian and New Zealand College of Psychiatrists and director of the New South Wales Institute of Psychiatry in Sydney, Australia. She is the convener of the Asylum Seekers Support Group of the RAN-ZCP and a member of the Health Professional Alliance for the Welfare of Asylum Seekers.

Jaap Orth, M.A., RMT (Dutch Association of Arts Therapists), has worked as a music therapist at the Phoenix Department of the psychiatric hospital, De Gelderse Roos, Wolfheze, the Netherlands since 1982. He is a committee member of Sirius, a foundation for methodology development, training, and support of art therapists who work with refugees and asylum seekers. He has presented lectures and workshops, and has published about music therapy and trauma. Presently he is running a research project on the effects of music therapy on psychopathology of the refugees and asylum seeker clients in treatment at the Phoenix Department.

Inge Roozen works as an art therapist in a special school for children with physical handicaps. She is also an expert in art education and as such develops programs, methodology, and exhibitions in the field of visual art.

Karin Schouten is a registered art therapist and artist. She is working with refugees and asylum seekers in a clinical setting of the Phoenix Department of De Gelderse Roos Mental Health Hospital in Wolfheze, the Netherlands. Currently she is setting up pilot projects for art therapy with female refugee groups and families. She is chairman of the art therapy division of the Dutch Association for Creative Arts Therapists (NVCT).

Derrick Silove, FRANZCP, M.D., is professor of psychiatry at the University of New South Wales, Sydney, Australia; director of the Psychiatry Research and Teaching Unit, South Western Sydney Area Health Service and Centre for Population Mental Health Research; psychiatrist at the Service for the Treatment and Rehabilitation of Torture Survivors, New South Wales; and project director of the East Timor National Mental Health Project.

Zachary Steel is a clinical psychologist and senior lecturer at the Centre for Population Mental Health Research at Liverpool Hospital, NSW Australia. He has worked with refugee and asylum seeker populations since 1992 and has published widely in medical journals, with his colleague Derrick Silove, documenting the psychological impact of harsh government policies on asylum seekers. Zachary has been involved in working for asylum seekers in a multitude of ways, including clinical research, medico-legal assessments, individual counseling, raising community awareness, media commentary, and support for refugee advocates and visiting detainees. His work with asylum seekers was recognized with a human rights commendation from the Australian Human Rights and Equal Opportunity Commission in 1992.

Silvana Turković, Ph.D., is a psychologist/psychotherapist working since 1986 with migrants and refugees in the Netherlands. She was attached to the Centrum '45/De Vonk, Dutch National Centre for treatment of victims of war. Since 2000 she has been affiliated with the Day Treatment

Centre for Asylum Seekers and Refugees/GGz's-Hertogenbosch and has been treating severely traumatized victims of war and political violence. She has also participated in projects of Medecins sans Frontieres and other NGOs in different post-war areas.

Stuart W. Turner is a consultant psychiatrist currently in private practice in London, honorary senior lecturer at the University College London, past president of the European Society for Traumatic Stress Studies, and current board member of the International Society for Traumatic Stress Studies. He is chair of trustees of the Refugee Therapy Centre, London and trustee of Redress, working for reparation for survivors of torture. He has been engaged in research with refugees over many years including the large-scale epidemiological survey of refugees in the UK and projects exploring specific aspects of the refugee experience (including the issue of memory and discrepancies).

Guus van der Veer is a psychologist/psychotherapist currently affiliated with the War Trauma Foundation in the Netherlands. He has broad experience in working with asylum seekers andrefugees, both in the Netherlands working at Pharos Foundation, and all over the world developing programs for *Medecins sans Frontieres*. He is the author of the book *Counselling and Therapy with Refugees* (Wiley), and contributor to numerous other books and scientific publications.

Marion van Dijk has been a practicing as art therapist since 1986 in a general clinical setting. Since 1996 she has been working at the Day Treatment Centre for Asylum Seekers and Refugees/GGz's-Hertogenbosch, the Netherlands. She has developed a special art therapy program for traumatized war and torture victims. Recently she has conducted a training program for *Medecins sans Frontieres*.

Jelly van Essen, M.D., is a psychotherapist. She is currently working for De Vonk Amsterdam, an outpatient clinic of Foundation Centrum '45, Treatment of and Research into the Consequences of Organized Violence, and she is associated with Pharos, Knowledge Centre for Refugees and Health, Utrecht, the Netherlands. She completed her medical studies in Amsterdam and had psychotherapeutic training in psychoanalytic psychotherapy and family therapy.

Adeline van Waning, M.D., Ph.D., is a psychiatrist/psychotherapist and staff member at the Netherlands Psychoanalytic Institute, and coordinator of the Working Group Intercultural Cooperation — psychoanalytic psychotherapy with migrants and refugees. She is also author and editor of several books and articles on multicultural society and psychoanalysis.

Jack Verburgt, M.A., RMT (Dutch Association of Arts Therapists), studied social sciences at the University of Nijmegen (the Netherlands) and music therapy at the Conservatory of Enschede. He has worked as a teacher and music therapist in two psychiatric hospitals since 1989, where he specialized in music therapy with personality disorders, depression, and PTSD. In these years he presented lectures and workshops and published about diagnostic and therapeutic issues.

Vamık D. Volkan, M.D., is emeritus professor of psychiatry at the University of Virginia, Charlottesville, and emeritus training and supervising analyst at the Washington Psychoanalytic Institute in Washington, D.C. He is also the Erik Erikson Scholar at the Austen Riggs Center, Stockbridge, Massachusetts and author of 30 books on clinical or psychopolitical topics.

Cecilia Wadensjö is a senior lecturer and researcher at the Department of Communication Studies, Linköping University, Sweden. She is also a state certified interpreter between Swedish and Russian. Her previous publications on the subject of interpreting include *Interpreting as Interaction* (Longman, 1998).

Joachim Walter, M.D., is a child and adolescent psychiatrist, psychoanalytical family therapist, and pediatrician. Currently he is the medical director of Child and Adolescent Psychiatry and Psychotherapy, Luisenklinik, Bad Dürrheim, Germany. He has been working with and for refugee families since 1981, and has established the outpatient clinic for refugee children and their families at the University Clinics of Eppendorf, Hamburg, where he has been working for twelve years. His main areas of publishing and research have been refugee children and families, intercultural therapy, and family therapy.

Titus Wertheim-Cahen is an art and occupational therapist with more then twenty-five years of clinical experience with traumatized adults, mostly child survivors of the World War II. She has initiated creative arts therapy programs for refugees and their children, and acts as an advisor to several humanitarian aid organizations. Recently she was appointed honorary member of the Dutch Association for Creative Arts Therapists because of her pioneering work in art therapy with war victims and refugees.

Acknowledgments

There are many people to whom we wish to extend our gratitude and thanks for assisting in making this book a reality. First, at Brunner-Routledge, a special thank you to publishing director George Zimmar for his dedication to the mission of this book; to enhance our knowledge of the consequences of political victimization which has resulted in over 35 million people worldwide becoming asylum seekers, refugees, torture, and war victims.

Second, our thanks to GGz's-Hertogenbosch/Outpatient and Day Treatment Centre for Refugees in the Netherlands for inviting one of the editors (John P. Wilson) to be a visiting scholar and to lecture on psychological trauma and PTSD. It was through that opportunity that Dr. Wilson met and began collaborating on this book project with Dr. Boris Droždek.

Third, thanks extend to Vamık Volkan for his insightful and moving introductory chapter which sets the tone for this volume. His passion and compassion are reflected by the contributions to this book by all of the authors.

Fourth, we would personally like to thank our families for supporting us and saving their wishes and plans for later while we were working on this project.

Finally, we extend deep gratitude to Ms. Kathleen Letizio, assistant to Professor Wilson, who oversaw the entire book preparation from beginning to end. Her dedication and willingness to go beyond the call of duty on many occasions ensured the timely completion of this book.

John P. Wilson
Boris Droždek

Preface

Broken Spirits in an Era of Trauma, Terrorism, and Globalization

BORIS DROŽĐEK AND JOHN P. WILSON

Broken Spirits is a book about this world, the world around us, and the crevices of society where asylum seekers and refugees exist. *Broken Spirits* is a metaphor for 40 million people worldwide who are victims of war, political oppression, and torture in all their insidious forms and humanly devised demonic variations. This book is about some aspects of life in this world. It is a book about disenfranchised people whose lives are dominated on a daily basis by fear, shame, guilt, and terrorized by nightmares, flashbacks, or unwanted memories of painful, life-threatening experiences they have been through. It is about individuals wrestling with feelings of hate and love, searching for safety, trust, and respect somewhere in the world, far from their homes. It is about people who were confronted with evil and who tried to rebuild their lives in unknown, new surroundings, facing another culture, language, norms, and values. It is about existence in societies indifferent to their destitution and marginal lives. This book tells the stories of millions of asylum-seeking people in this world, even though we deny or forget that worldwide there are 40 million such people, many with families in this abyss of existence.

Broken Spirits is also a book about mental health workers all over the world, in countries of asylum and in war zones, assisting the victims of war, political violence, and torture. It is about their experiences and knowledge. It is about their coping with powerlessness and the daily despair of their clients. It is about the passion and compassion they have for their work. It is about the fatigue they feel, but also about the refueling beauty of encounters they have with others who ask for help but at the same time have power to share, the power of the spirit that only survivors can display.

WHY READ *BROKEN SPIRITS?*

The worldwide mental health problems and psychological needs of traumatized asylum seekers and refugees are public health issues. The knowledge about this population and their needs is surprisingly not widespread. It seems that a conspiracy of silence surrounds this topic of traumatized asylum seekers who want freedom from tyranny and political oppression. We all know that evil and suffering exist, but even when the victims become part of our reality, we try to deny the immense impact this palpable evil has had on their lives. The societal awareness of the vast array of the problems and needs of asylum seekers and refugees is very low. Ignorance and denial prevail and are ubiquitously present even among professional mental health workers. In many countries in the world, different social and political strategies are actively used to discourage asylum seekers from entering a country and applying for protection and security. As a consequence, traumatized victims of torture or political and war-related violence do not get the protection they need and float adrift caught between rigid government bureaucracies and nowhere to go.

At the same time impressive advances have been made in the provision of innovative mental health services for traumatized asylum seekers and refugees. Unfortunately, they have not yet been systematically and widely known to mental health providers and professionals (e.g., general practitioners, lawyers, psychiatrists, psychologists, social workers, etc.) working in this field in different parts of the world. Well-intentioned professionals, paralyzed by the geographical and psychological proximity of evil and who carefully document it, ask themselves what they are supposed to do to help their clients. Other refugee workers are busy developing very sophisticated treatment strategies and continue to improve them. But there is little communication of those efforts to others who could help the immense problems of asylum seekers, namely, politicians, legislators, and leaders of the free world.

This book is a comprehensive international handbook that presents theoretical considerations and practical guidelines for the treatment of traumatized asylum seekers and refugees. A wealth of experience has been collected and generated on this topic in the past 10 years. This book aims at structuring this knowledge and communicating it with case workers, academics, and policymakers throughout the world.

ABOUT *BROKEN SPIRITS*

Broken Spirits is a book focusing on complex psychological sequelae that asylum seekers and refugees, being exposed to multiple traumatic events in the context of war and political violence, followed by forced migration, and postmigratory secondary victimization, suffer from on a daily basis.

In Part I, a broad spectrum of theoretical, conceptual, and sociocultural considerations is presented. The issues of forced migration, torture, and political violence are discussed as well as their relationship to mental health issues. The assessment of asylum seekers' and refugees' mental health problems and the role of culture in diagnosis and treatment, the so-called cultural validity and responsibility, are discussed as well.

Part II focuses on the impact of traumatic injuries to the individual level of the Self. Public mental health and cultural aspects of massive traumatization are presented in the way that theoretical considerations are intertwined with examples from fieldwork.

In Parts III, IV, and V of the book, authors discuss a broad spectrum of treatment issues and provide guidelines for practitioners. Part III focuses on verbal therapies in different forms—individual and group, supportive, and trauma focused. There are also chapters on other relevant topics like creation of a therapeutic alliance, treatment with use of interpreters, transference and countertransference issues, and how to organize clinical supervision for caretakers in order to prevent secondary traumatization and burnout. Part IV offers guidelines for those practicing nonverbal or experiential therapies. A choice has been made among many existing forms of nonverbal approaches and four of them are presented in depth: psychomotor therapy, body psychotherapy, art therapy, and music therapy. They are of great use in assisting asylum seekers and refugees due to communication difficulties and the fact that trauma sometimes leaves the victims speechless. Part V provides guidelines for treatment of special populations. Gender-specific issues as well as relevant topics in assisting children and adolescents are presented.

Part VI offers an overview of experiences and possibilities in psychopharmacology and psychosocial rehabilitation of traumatized asylum seekers and refugees. Medical and surgical complications in work with torture victims and patients with posttraumatic stress disorder (PTSD) are discussed.

Part VII focuses on legal, ethical, and political perspectives of work with asylum seekers and refugees. In dealing with this disenfranchised population, mental health workers are confronted not only with consequences of the clients' psychological breakdown, but the limitations and breakdown of social and governmental systems. Advocacy is considered to be an integral part of treatment, and authors provide practical guidelines in legal assistance and political support.

The mission of this book is to collect, organize, and update knowledge in the field that has proliferated worldwide and present it in a compact form for use in education, research, and health care delivery systems. Beyond this framework, future research and clinical innovations are not only possible but an urgent necessity.

Theoretical, Conceptual, and Sociocultural Considerations

Theoretical, Conceptual, and Sociocultural Considerations

Introduction

JOHN P. WILSON

Part I of this book contains five chapters; the first is an introduction by Vamık Volkan. These chapters present theoretical, conceptual, and sociocultural considerations for working with asylum seekers, refugees, and war and torture victims. As such, they establish a foundational framework by which to understand the complex and difficult work with people who have been uprooted from their homelands and thrust into the very uncertain world of seeking shelter, political status, and a niche in another country and culture. Asylum seekers, refugees, and war and torture victims have been cast adrift on the seas of fate and the mercy of God. As victims of war, political upheaval, or catastrophe, they journey from a home base of known certainties to unknown places in an unfamiliar culture. It is a process of uprooting, being dislodged from established patterns of daily living, and having a meaningful role in a community. The process of becoming, and later being, an asylum seeker and refugee is difficult at best and often traumatizing. However, the traumatizing effects of asylum seeking or being a refugee in a homeland or "strangeland" are overlayed by personal experiences of trauma. Many asylum seekers and refugees have layers of trauma — personal, familial, social, cultural, national, and spiritual. They bring the legacy of their own trauma experiences and personal losses (e.g., loved ones, home, family, country, job) with them to the country in which they seek acceptance and opportunities to build new lives with a tangible hope for a better future. For many, the journey from leaving homeland to becoming an asylum seeker is a journey of travel into psychological uncertainty and the darkness of the unknown that is experienced as living "in between" different worlds of reality; that which "was" and that which "exists" without a foreseeable future. Psychologically, it is the peril of the abyss (see Wilson, Chapter 6).

In the introductory chapter, Vamık Volkan presents a broad overview of the issues facing refugees and asylum seekers. He emphasizes the political processes within and between countries and their consequences for the lives of ordinary people who become the "pawns" and victims of malevolent political forces. Among the many themes discussed in the chapter, Volkan points out that issues of personal identity are paramount for asylum seekers. The identity question of "Who am I?" reigns at center stage in the course of adaptation. Asylum seeking and refugee status challenge the foundational basis of having a sense of self-sameness and continuity, for such feelings rapidly dissipate upon forced migration, dislocation, and the process of finding a new life and sense of meaning in an alien environment. The author notes that feelings of guilt over *loss* of parts of the self (i.e., the immigrant's or the refugee's previous identity, his or her investment in the language, culture, land, and people left behind, etc.) can complicate the mourning process. By identifying the presence of guilt reactions, the author correctly notes that they are linked to other psychological processes, which include depression, identity confusion, shame, helplessness, and culture shock. Moreover, culture shock embraces a large domain of adaptive processes, including emotional reactions of anxiety, depression, fear, uncertainty, anger, and rage. Culture shock also includes feelings of mourning for the lost culture but also the discomfort in understanding and adapting to a different culture. Volkan makes note that there is a form of culture shock known to mental health professionals who come from the "outside" to visit the misery of persons in refugee camps who are freshly traumatized. He also notes that the "outsider" brings his *assumptive professional beliefs* with him to the squalor and destruction of the camps and conceives of plans of intervention and assistance. But are these plans based on the assumptive beliefs of the "outsider" like trying to put a square peg into a round hole? In many cases, the answer is yes and illustrates that in working with asylum seekers and refugees, dual realities of understanding exist, those of help seekers and those of helpers in a role of power and influence who can direct the course of action taken on behalf of dislocated, uprooted, and disenfranchised persons seeking life in a new country. The themes illustrated by Volkan in the introductory chapter are amplified and developed in the subsequent chapters in Part I.

In Chapter 2, Derrick Silove provides perspectives on the global challenge of asylum seekers. This chapter provides an historical overview of the many issues associated with culturally displaced persons. This historical perspective places in relief the fact that refugees have always existed and, as such, present enduring and recurring problems to the host country. First, refugees have been used by host countries as advisors, double-agents (espionage), negotiators, slaves, indentured servants, and prostitutes. Second, refugees are often Janus-faced toward their host country, being seen as victims and heroes as well as intruders and leeches. This view of refugees reflects attitudes of ambivalence among those responsible for them in the host country. Silove traces the evolution of social policy and attitudes toward health care services and notes that the most significant advances were made post–World War II and the advent of the Holocaust. Among these historical developments was the growth of the United Nations High Commission on Refugees (UNHCR) and other international agencies and nongovernmental agencies (NGOs) that were created or commissioned to provide assistance to refugees and victims of war and catastrophe. Silove correctly notes in his chapter that the availability of scientific literature on stress, trauma, and PTSD provided more adequate paradigms by which to evaluate the mental health needs of refugees. Moreover, since trauma encompasses many forms of extreme experiences, Silove documents that these include human rights abuse, torture, starvation, political internment, and warfare. Further, he highlights that traumatic events occur at communal and individual levels and create unique problems of coping and adaptation for refugees. Finally, Silove suggests that refugees need advocates for their welfare, and that systematic scientific research is needed to advance understanding of the complexities they confront.

In Chapter 3, Jens Modvig and James Jaranson succinctly review the substantial and diverse literature on the effects of torture and political violence. As they note in the introduction to their chapter, they seek to "(a) review political violence and torture, including the atrocities, global occurrence, and impact on the health of individuals and populations; (b) discuss definitions of torture and organized violence; (c) provide a broad account of types of violence; (d) present briefly the current knowledge regarding interactions between threats and their biopsychosocial response mechanisms; and (e) review the available data about torture and posttraumatic stress prevalence among victims of torture and related human rights violations." These stated objectives form the basis of the chapter and its contents. In the way of a concise summary, Modvig and Jaranson provide a step-by-step guide to understanding. First, there is a useful glossary of key concepts (i.e., stressor, traumatic event, violence, etc.). Second, they discuss the categories of political violence by duration, intensity, and target level (e.g., individual versus group). Third, they provide a condensed discussion of the methods of torture and their psychological consequences. Fourth, they review the studies on torture prevalence in different countries of the world. Finally, they discuss the mental health consequences of torture, including psychiatric disorders such as PTSD, depression, anxiety, and substance abuse.

In Chapter 4, Jorge Aroche and Mariano Coello provide a discussion of ethnocultural considerations in treatment. Ethnocultural refers specifically to ethnic and cultural factors that are important to consider when devising social policies and health care programs for refugees. Ethnocultural factors include culture of origin, values, beliefs, rituals, practices, and assumptive worldview ideological systems. As the authors note in reference to communal and individual trauma, "[it] is not a disembodied construct, as suggested by DSM-IV, it is a cultural and historical reality that must be entered into by the clinician." Given this framework, the authors discuss trauma and PTSD *within* an embedded cultural perspective and note that "most of the problems commonly exhibited by refugee and asylum seekers are the result of a dynamic interaction between trauma-related or posttraumatic issues, the stresses and demands of exile, migration and resettlement process, and other stressors that affect refugees much in the same way as they affect the rest of the population." Having noted the dynamic interplay between sociocultural and individual factors in determining mental health outcomes, the authors delineate the ways to overcome barriers to effective service delivery.

The last chapter in Part I concerns the important question of the assessment of PTSD and dual diagnosis in asylum seekers and refugee patients. In Chapter 5, Alexander McFarlane concisely presents an overview of the critical factors that must be considered by professionals working with asylum seekers and refugees and who must make multiaxial diagnoses per the DSM-IV or ICD-10 DCR.

McFarlane's chapter raises important issues for consideration when making clinical assessments and diagnoses. We can list a few of these conceptual and clinical dilemmas in the form of questions: How do the culture and worldview of the patient affect how he or she processes and understands traumatic experiences? How do religious beliefs affect the processing and reporting of trauma (e.g., a Buddhist's belief in states of karma)? How do ethnocultural beliefs affect the interpretation of extremely stressful experiences (e.g., "really strong men do not get PTSD in this culture")? How does one adequately assess symptoms in culturally diverse clients? How does one use tools developed in Western countries for clients from non-Western countries?

In his chapter, McFarlane discusses many of the questions raised above. Moreover, he provides both a discussion and a table that shows the comparison between the DSM-IV and ICD-10 DCR diagnostic criteria for PTSD. This table allows international comparisons to be made for practitioners working in different cultural settings. Finally, McFarlane notes in agreement with Silove that "to leave psychiatric disorders such as depression and PTSD undiagnosed and untreated represents a considerable source of burden of suffering to the individual."

1

From Hope for a Better Life to Broken Spirits: An Introduction

VAMIK D. VOLKAN

BROKEN SPIRITS: A TIMELY AND TIMELESS TOPIC

After the collapse of the Soviet Union and the end of the Cold War, former U.S. President George Bush, Sr., introduced the idea of a "New World Order" and envisioned "kinder and gentler" times. This vision, as we all know, has by no means materialized. Massive human tragedies deliberately caused by "others," people also usually known as "enemies," occurred during and after his presidency, resulting in, among other disasters, tens of thousands of refugees and asylum seekers. Little more than a decade later, the former president's son, George Bush, Jr. — and of course all of us — are more than ever aware of a "new" kind of international aggression, worldwide terrorism, and a "new" kind of ruthless response to it. The fact is that, when we do not deny it, we realize that the human psychology of individuals or large groups has not changed; what *is* changing with great speed is the mastery of technological challenges, which, among other things, has created more and more destructive weapons.

Humans will continue maiming and killing other humans, ruining their environments, and even destroying priceless art forms like those

7

from the Bamian Valley in Afghanistan or in the National Museum of
Baghdad, especially when such art forms are perceived as belonging to
"others" or "enemies." Humans will flee from massive disasters, thousands and millions will face forced immigration, and their spirits will,
finally, be broken.

Anyone who visits one of the many refugee camps in the world
today and truly listens to the stories of refugees and asylum seekers
cannot deny the existence of aggression within human nature. Hearing from witnesses and victims what human beings are capable of
doing to others for the sake of advancing security or for protecting
their "large-group identity" (Volkan, 1997, 1999) only makes this
aggression more incontestable.

Focusing on human aggression, however, should not overshadow the
fact that humans also care for others, and that large groups seek not
only "enemies" but also "allies" (Volkan, 1988). Because we "love" others, we also wish to repair and restore them. Those of us in the mental
health field strive to understand those with broken spirits, to find methods of treatment, and to establish guidelines as a manifestation of the
"healing" side of human nature. The chapters included in this book
range from theoretical analyses of the psychological processes that refugees and asylum seekers experience to specific considerations, including
concern for translators who accompany outsider helpers and who may
become traumatized themselves. Understanding these issues necessi-
tates a look at one essential aspect of the refugee or asylum-seeker's
experience — dislocation.

Voluntary Dislocation

The external and internal worlds of voluntary immigrants are vastly different from that of refugees or asylum seekers. Nevertheless, there are
also common elements that underlie the psychology of both the
"normal" (voluntary) immigrant and the traumatized forced immigrant,
an asylum seeker, or a refugee. Since moving from one location to
another involves loss — loss of country, friends, and previous identity —
all dislocation experiences can be examined in terms of the immigrant's
ability to mourn and/or resist the mourning process. The extent to
which the individual is able intrapsychically to accept his or her loss will
determine the degree to which an adjustment is made to the new life
(Volkan, 1993).

Feelings of guilt over loss of parts of the self (i.e., the immigrant's or
the refugee's previous identity, his or her investment in the language,
land and people left behind, etc.) may complicate the immigrant's
mourning process. When guilt is "persecutory" — the individual is
driven by his or her guilt to expect punishment from others — the new-
comer becomes prone to pathological mourning. If the individual
acknowledges the loss of his or her past life intrapsychically and is able
to accept the pain (Kleinians call this "depressive guilt"), the individual

might exhibit sorrow, but he or she will still be able to retain reparative tendencies. The immigrant or refugee who has "depressive guilt" may be better equipped to adjust to a new life (Grinberg and Grinberg, 1989).

In the case of the refugee, the individual's own psychological organization generates more persecutory guilt than may be found in the individual who becomes an immigrant by choice. After all, the refugee's guilt is reinforced by his or her being a survivor, while relatives and friends remain in danger. If discrimination within the "host" society is faced by either the immigrant or the refugee, however, persecutory anxieties are kept alive and/or may be rekindled.

Garza-Guerrero (1974) states that initially, the immigrant experiences culture shock (Ticho, 1971) due to the sudden change from an "average expectable environment" — as described by Hartmann (1939/1958) — to a strange and unpredictable one. He or she may activate a fantasy that the past contained all "good" self- and object-representations, along with their gratifying affective links; when the reality of dislocation sets in, such representations are felt to be missing. At some point, the immigrant feels disconnected from his or her "good" object representations and experiences a sense of discontinuity. The initiation of the mourning process can change this feeling. Completion of mourning leads to identification with what had been lost. "Good" object representations that are lost now become internalized and thus the immigrant establishes an internal link between his or her past and present; his or her life experience now has "continuity."

If there are no complications — that is, if the individual primarily suffers from depressive, not persecutory guilt — the average immigrant can complete the work of mourning (Freud, 1917) that is necessary for human adaptation after a loss. Garza-Guerrero (1974) states that once the immigrant works through the mourning of what he or she has abandoned, the immigrant can form a new identity that is neither a total surrender to the new culture nor the sum of bicultural endowment. The new identity will be reflected in a remodeled self-representation that incorporates selective characteristics into the new culture that were harmoniously integrated or that proved congruent with the cultural heritage of the past.

If the immigrant still feels accepted in the country left behind, he or she, upon completion of the work of mourning, may experience biculturalism, resulting in a sense of belonging to neither culture to the exclusion of the other. In fact, he or she will belong "totally to both" (Julius, 1992, p. 56).

Whichever framework one uses to understand the adaptation of immigrants to dislocation, it is important to understand that many newcomers — especially if their dislocation experience occurs after puberty — become "perennial mourners" to one degree or another, perhaps because even well-adjusted immigrants retain some aspects of persecutory guilt (Volkan, 1993). Some images of what has been lost (family, land, identity) are *not* as relegated to the realm of futureless past memory as they are in "normal" mourning (Tähkä, 1993). In the latter case, after the mourner completes the work of mourning, what is left behind becomes only a memory. For example, the mourner does not imagine, with associated feelings, that a dead lover or a lover left in the old country will still satisfy his or her sexual wishes. The image of the lover becomes "futureless." A *perennial* mourner will behave as if lost objects have a future in his or her life. Many immigrants remain perennial mourners on a continuum that can be considered "usual" to "extreme."

Forced Dislocation

The voluntary immigration experience, itself, because it involves losses, is a traumatic experience. But *forced* immigration includes the effects of *actual* trauma, as is illustrated in this book again and again.

It is more difficult and often impossible for refugees and/or those who are exiled to complete the work of mourning. Their mourning processes are complicated due to actual traumatic experiences. One has to deal with the effects of the actual trauma before such an individual can become like ordinary, "normal" immigrants; if he or she is to genuinely begin the work of mourning: "it is necessary to reconnect with a repudiated past" (Wangh, 1992, p. 16). External factors are crucial in determining whether a refugee or an exile will be able to feel like an ordinary immigrant.

Although there is no need to add further examples of forced immigration here, I would like to bring attention to a situation in which people can become "refugees" even without moving from their own locations when, due to warlike conditions, wars, or oppression by conquering forces, the place where they live becomes "foreign" for them. Consider, for example, Krusha e Madhe, an agricultural village within the boundaries of Kosovo, very near to Albania. During the war in Kosovo, Serbs attacked the village of 5,200 people in 740 families. A little over 200 people were massacred, leaving 138 widows and 400 orphans. Many more were maimed and handicapped. There were incinerators in the village where most of the bodies of the massacre victims were burned. For years to come the widows and children awoke every morning to see the buildings in which the bodies of their murdered husbands, fathers, mothers, other relatives, and friends were burned to ashes. Naturally, their village had become a "foreign" land for them because the environment no longer induced feelings of home among the inhabitants. Another example is the village of Lovas in Croatia, on the border with Serbia near the city of Vukovar. Yugoslav army and Serb paramilitary groups, including their Serb neighbors, during the war have heavily massacred the Croatian population of the village. Croats left and became refugees in other parts of the country that were not as affected by the war. Serbs stayed in the village. Years later, when Croats were permitted to return permanently to the village and to their homes, they continued to live among their "old" Serb neighbors, as if the war had never happened. But it felt just partially like "home." Meeting their neighbors daily, the Croats were constantly triggered for their traumatic memories.

A Split in Mental Health Workers' Response to Refugees

Along with considering the internal world of refugees and asylum seekers, the authors in this book rightly consider and explore the internal world of mental health workers as well, especially those who are not refugees or asylum seekers themselves. When mental health workers from an outside, safe world go to meet refugees or asylum seekers in the countries from where they escaped, in miserable refugee camps or in the refugees' original homes that have become "foreign" for the inhabitants, they usually develop an elevated version of a kind of *splitting*. On one hand, outsider mental health workers hold on to their professional identities, consider theories about trauma, mourning, and adaptation, and, based on their training and experience, plan therapeutic strategies for the victims; this is the "intellectual" side of splitting. On the other hand, these mental health workers identify, at least temporarily, with refugees and asylum seekers in order to communicate with them on an emotional level. The same phenomenon occurs, in maybe less pregnant form, when one works with asylum seekers and refugees in his or her own country.

Traumatized asylum seekers and refugees, however, have gone through life experiences that are beyond the life experiences of the caretakers. The contributors to this book, outside caregivers, when writing about theories, treatment strategies, and providing guidelines also directly or indirectly illustrate their empathic identifications with their patients and the forming of human relationships. Most of them clearly have found an appropriate balance between the two sides of the split that necessarily occurs when dealing with patients who have suffered such traumatic experiences.

This book is thought to be a textbook for anyone who plans to be therapeutically involved not only with "normal" voluntary refugees, but also and especially with traumatized ones. Considering what is going on in the world at the present time, this book is also timely. What is described within its covers is also timeless, however, because in the future too, massive human aggression will undoubtedly continue, and we will then be faced with the need for therapeutic strategies to care for new waves of refugees and asylum seekers.

REFERENCES

Freud, S. (1917). Mourning and melancholia. *Standard Edition, 14,* 237–260.
Garza-Guerrero, A. C. (1974). Culture shock: Its mourning and vicissitudes of identity. *Journal of the American Psychoanalytic Association, 22,* 400–429.

Grinberg, L. and Grinberg, R. (1989). *Psychoanalytic Perspectives on Migration and Exile*, tr. N. Festinger. New Haven, CT: Yale University Press.

Hartmann, H. (1958). *Ego psychology and problems of adaptation*. New York: International Universities Press. (Original work published 1939.)

Julius, D. A. (1992). Biculturalism and international interdependence. *Mind and Human Interaction, 3*, 53–56.

Tähkä, V. (1993). *Mind and its treatment: A psychoanalytic approach*. Madison, CT: International Universities Press.

Ticho, G. (1971). Cultural aspects of transference and countertransference. *Bulletin of the Menniger Clinic, 35*, 313–334.

Volkan, V. D. (1988). *The need to have enemies and allies: From clinical practice to international relationships*. Northvale, NJ: Jason Aronson.

Volkan, V. D. (1993). Immigrants and refugees: A psychodynamic perspective. *Mind and Human Interaction, 4*, 63–75.

Volkan, V. D. (1997). *Bloodlines: From ethnic pride to ethnic terrorism*. New York: Farrar, Straus, & Giroux.

Volkan, V. D. (1999). Psychoanalysis and diplomacy part I: Individual and large group identity. *Journal of Applied Psychoanalytic Studies, 1*, 29–55.

Wangh, M. (1992, Winter). Being a refugee and being an immigrant. *International Psychoanalysis*, 15–17.

2

The Global Challenge of Asylum

DERRICK SILOVE

> While spurning refugees we are hell-bent on creating more of them.
>
> **Anonymous**

INTRODUCTION

Since the beginning of the 1990s, an escalation in conflict around the world has generated refugee flows of a scale that has been unprecedented since World War II (Amnesty International, 2002). Yet, at the very time of this asylum crisis, mental health professionals are facing new challenges in assisting displaced persons exposed to mass violence. After the terrorist attacks on the United States on September 11, 2001, there has been a perceptible shift in the commitment to human rights amongst leading world nations, a regression rationalized by the "war against terror" (Silove, 2003; Summerfield, 2003).

Even prior to September 11, there had been a steady erosion of the regime of humane protection offered to asylum seekers, with policies of deterrence leading to conditions of deprivation and confinement of displaced persons in recipient countries (Silove, Ekblad, & Mollica, 2000; Watters, 1998). Within the mental health profession itself, controversy has erupted about the value of psychological interventions offered to refugees and postconflict populations, particularly when provided by Western-trained professionals (Eyber & Ager, 2002; Summerfield, 1999). In order to understand the context in which these challenges have evolved and to consider strategies to confront them, it is necessary to review recent trends in the history of mass conflict and refugee flows.

HISTORICAL OVERVIEW

Throughout the ages, forcibly displaced persons have occupied a vulnerable status in recipient societies, with their precarious claims to residency rights creating a fertile ground for exploitation, marginalization, and expulsion (Silove, 2002a). For example, during the wars between Attila the Hun and the Roman Empire, refugees variously were scapegoated, enslaved, or held hostage. As in other times in history, refugees were also used as go-betweens, advisors, and double agents. By confining refugees to particular roles, such as usurers and tax collectors in the case of the Jews of Europe in the Middle Ages, stigma was affixed to ethnic minorities, making them ready scapegoats during times of civil unrest.

In other historical epochs, when liberated from institutional restrictions, refugees have played pivotal roles in the development of host societies, acting as catalysts for major social transformations. Emancipated Jews were instrumental in the advancement of the Austro-Hungarian empire, and refugees and other immigrants played a transforming role in creating the pluralistic societies of North America and Australasia after the mass migrations from Europe in the early and mid-20th century.

This pattern of historical flux in the fortunes of refugees through the ages illustrates a key point (Silove, 2002a): where refugees have been welcomed and offered opportunities to develop their capacities and to participate in all the affairs of the host country, they have overcome major adversities of the past. In contrast, where refugees are marginalized, victimized, or constrained, they tend to become entrapped in negative stereotypic roles that are self-reinforcing, leading to further persecution and deprivation. This Janus face of the refugee, at times seen as hero and at others as intruder, continues to be evident in the modern history of displacement.

The Golden Age of Humanitarian Concern

The early post–World War II era was a particularly enlightened period in relation to the treatment of refugees worldwide. Collective shame about the failure of leading nations to protect victims of the Nazi Holocaust galvanized world leaders in the postwar period to develop international humanitarian instruments aimed at protecting persecuted and displaced populations worldwide. These obligations were enshrined in the Geneva Refugee Convention (1951), a covenant that was extended globally by the Protocol of 1967 (Courtland Robinson, 1998). For the first time, the rights of refugees were clearly enunciated and embodied in international humanitarian law. Signatory nations were obliged to give safe haven to persons who, for reasons of race, religion, political affiliation, or belief systems had a "well-founded" fear of returning to their countries of origin (Courtland Robinson, 1998).

In the following 25 years, the Convention served refugees well. During the Cold War, dissidents fleeing from totalitarian nations were welcomed in the West. The numbers were relatively small, displaced persons were European and often well educated, and the spirit of generosity was promoted at a communal level by Cold War ideology. Refugees from the USSR, Hungary, Czechoslovakia, and other Eastern Bloc countries were given permanent residency and were rapidly integrated into host societies.

Shift in Public Opinion and Policy

The mid-1970s signaled a radical change in the world refugee situation (Courtland Robinson, 1998). When the wars in Indochina ended with communist takeovers of Vietnam, Cambodia, and Laos, large numbers of refugees fled across the borders into neighboring countries of Southeast Asia or by boat to more distant destinations, including Australia. For the first time since World War II, the flow of displaced persons numbered in the hundreds of thousands (Mollica et al., 1993).

The sequence of international responses that this mass migration evoked is noteworthy, since the pattern has been repeated ever since. The first Vietnamese refugees, often educated supporters of Western influence in Indochina, were offered permanent resettlement in countries such as Australia and the United States. As the numbers swelled, however, attitudes of traditional recipient countries hardened (Courtland Robinson, 1998). Large numbers of Indochinese were held for prolonged periods in refugee camps in countries of first asylum, in conditions of social instability and deprivation. As the crisis continued, particularly in locations such as Hong Kong, the refugee camp was transformed into the detention center, cramped, bleak, prisonlike institutions in which allegations of human rights abuses were widespread.

The political rhetoric accompanying these shifts in policy underwent several transformations. In the early phase, Indochinese refugees were seen as heroes since they supported the Western mission in Southeast Asia. As time progressed, they were subjected to increasingly stringent screening procedures in refugee camps in order to determine who were "real" refugees (Courtland Robinson, 1998). Finally, the focus of geopolitics turned to solutions of repatriation rather than resettlement, a reflection of "refugee fatigue," with Western governments turning away from a problem that was no longer driven by any social, political, economic, or strategic imperatives.

War and Refugee Policies Since the 1990s

Since the 1990s, modern conflicts have typically occurred in postcolonial nations with short legacies of statehood, a relative absence of functional democratic institutions, entrenched patterns of corruption, and within a social matrix of ethnic and religious diversity. State authority typically has been weak, and in some instances, governing institutions have disintegrated to the point of lawlessness. Infrastructure and services barely exist in such failed states, and much of the population live in conditions of extreme poverty.

The low-grade wars that have erupted in such settings around the globe have provoked a crisis of asylum that has grown to unprecedented proportions since the early 1990s. Over that period, the number of refugees worldwide has ranged from 14 to 16 million, a threefold increase since the 1980s (UNHCR, 2001). There are even more internally displaced persons (22 million) creating a total uprooted population of some 35 million worldwide (World Refugee Survey, 2003). The internally displaced (IDP) are out of reach of international humanitarian agencies that are mandated to provide protection only to refugees who cross national borders. By far the majority of refugees and IDPs are located in low-income countries of Asia, the Middle East, Africa, and Latin America (Amnesty International, 2002). Of the 20 nations with the highest density of displaced persons residing within their borders, the only Western nation represented, Canada, ranks 19th (Amnesty International, 2002).

Regional civil wars continue to generate large refugee flows. Conflicts in Sudan, Colombia, Sri Lanka, and East Timor, to name but a few countries, typically have been low-grade, nonconventional wars waged by liberation movements, separatist groups, or militia, in which civilians have been the major casualties. Human rights violations on a mass scale, although ubiquitous in previous wars, have become central to the conduct of such conflicts. Genocidal strategies, often rationalized by ancient religious and ethnic enmities, commonly are used by elites to exert and maintain their control of resources and political power.

Adding to the pressures of forced migration, torture continues to be used in over 100 countries worldwide (Amnesty International, 2002) not only by state authorities but by militia and other nonstate actors. Widespread availability of easily operated, yet lethal weapons such as semiautomatic rifles, rocket-launched grenades, and landmines has made it possible for the effective prosecution of warfare by drug lords, chieftains, militia, and other nonstate groupings. Forced recruitment of children as soldiers, mass rape of women, manipulation of aid, and the creation of concentration and slave labor camps have become the stock-in-trade instruments of war, not only to achieve physical dominance, but also as weapons of mass psychological control and intimidation (Amnesty International, 2002).

THE CHANGING FACE OF THE REFUGEE

The sheer scale of the world problem of war and displacement, the cultural, religious, and political remoteness of affected populations from Western societies, and the seeming intractability of these conflicts all add to the reluctance of traditional refugee recipient societies to receive increasing numbers of displaced persons.

September 11, 2001, signaled another decisive crossroad, one of the unseen casualties being the erosion of the commitment by some Western nations to the international human rights regime built over the preceding 50 years (Silove, 2003; Summerfield, 2003). In the public mind, the war against terrorism has become confused with the challenge posed by asylum seekers, a blurring of issues seemingly fostered by political rhetoric. In reality, the two groups, terrorists and asylum seekers, are at opposite poles of the spectrum, and any confusion of the two reflects an age-old tendency to blame the victim. A reflection of the paradox created by such political rhetoric is that Iraqi asylum seekers fleeing torture and persecution continued to languish in detention centers in Australia at the very time that the host country engaged in war to liberate Iraqis from the oppressive Saddam Hussein regime.

In a context of growing public fear of outsiders, particularly those from different cultures and religious backgrounds, it has not been difficult for politicians in Western countries to argue in favor of closing the doors to asylum seekers. Those arriving spontaneously at the borders of Western countries are labeled as queue jumpers, displacing "legitimate" refugees who apply off-shore to enter the country (Silove et al., 2000). That characterization is belied by the facts: in many of the countries that produce asylum flows, access to embassies is limited or nonexistent, making it impossible for the persecuted to obtain refugee documents prior to their flight (Silove et al., 2000). Contrary to claims made by politicians that most asylum seekers are opportunistic intruders seeking economic betterment, there is growing evidence that this subgroup might constitute the most traumatized of the wider refugee population (see below). Seeking asylum is not a crime according to international law — indeed, the Refugee Convention (1951) explicitly entitles persecuted persons to seek such sanctuary.

Yet asylum seekers have been targeted for harsh and restrictive measures (Bunce, 1997) in order to "send a message" to discourage compatriots overseas from following the path of those who have fled (Silove et al., 2000). Several Western governments have pursued draconian policies of deterrence, including the interdiction of ships carrying refugees, forced repatriation without adequate assessment of refugee claims, and denial of access to basic services to those who manage to gain entry into the intended country of resettlement.

Australia, a country that has received far fewer asylum seekers than other Western nations, has instituted some of the most rigid policies, particularly the long-term, mandatory detention without legal review of asylum seekers, including women and children, in remote centers far from compatriot populations (Silove et al., 2000). More recently, that country has diverted shiploads of asylum seekers to impoverished Pacific island nations (the so-called Pacific solution), where many continue to languish in poorly serviced detention centers. From a mental health perspective, these regressive policies have posed several new dilemmas, including questions about the wider role of mental health professionals in advocating for humane policies in dealing with displaced persons (Silove, 2002a).

TRAUMA AND STRESS IN ASYLUM SEEKERS AND REFUGEES

Yet, within this broader context of harsh treatment of asylum seekers, controversy persists among mental health professionals about the need for interventions for these persons. On the one hand, the science of refugee mental health has made substantial strides in recent times (Mollica et al., 2001), with a substantial number of epidemiological studies being published in the field (de Jong et al., 2001; Lopes Cardozo, Vergara, Agani, & Gotway, 2000; Mollica et al., 1993, 1999). At the same time, critics have questioned whether traumatic stress, as conceptualized by Western-trained professionals, has any relevance to postconflict communities and refugees from other cultures (Eyber & Ager, 2002; Summerfield, 1999). In particular, doubts have been raised as to whether psychiatric categories such as posttraumatic stress disorder (PTSD) reflect anything more than normative psychological reactions that do not incur any psychosocial disability (Summerfield, 1999). The inference drawn is that Western-derived trauma counseling is unwarranted, ineffective, and culturally alien to many refugee groups (Eyber & Ager, 2002).

Given these serious challenges to the field, it is timely to reassess critically what is known about refugee trauma, whether traumatic stress should always be the focus of interventions for refugee and postconflict societies, and whether it is possible to formulate a consensual framework for intervention that encompasses a broader range of relevant issues that affect displaced persons.

Human Rights Abuses Among Refugees and Asylum Seekers

An area of consensus is the extent to which displaced persons have been subjected to human rights abuses. A growing body of research has shown that displaced persons claiming refugee status have experienced extensive exposure to torture, gross human rights violations, death of family members, and other major traumas. Such reports have emanated from different cultural settings and contexts worldwide (de Jong et al., 2001; Mollica et al., 1993, 1998; Steel, Silove, Bird, McGorry, & Mohan, 1999), reaffirming the principle that the common motivation underpinning refugee flight is the need to escape from extreme danger and persecution.

Immigration officials regularly challenge the histories of persecution presented by asylum seekers, and the secrecy with which torture and related abuses are perpetrated make verification of individual trauma stories difficult. Nevertheless, clinicians working in the field rarely have cause to doubt the trauma stories recounted by refugees, with their accounts being consistent with historical conditions known to pertain in their countries of origin. A recent study has confirmed that, although details often are forgotten, recall of major abuses recorded by refugees remains consistent over time (Herlihy, Scragg, & Turner, 2002).

Hence, the problem of credibility relates less to the genuine experiences of persecution experienced by refugees than to the politically motivated attitudes of immigration officials assessing their claims. The process of assessing asylum claims is often adversarial, with asylum seekers becoming distressed and at times incoherent during the proceedings. The consequence can be that their fragmented or contradictory testimony is attributed erroneously to fabrication rather than to underlying memory disturbances and dissociation caused by traumatic stress reactions.

The Mental Health of Refugees and Asylum Seekers

In the contemporary geopolitical context, therefore, it becomes particularly important to represent the mental health of refugees accurately. If displaced persons are depicted as chronically psychologically disabled, then recipient countries might argue that admitting larger quotas of refugees will impose excessive costs on state resources (Silove & Ekblad, 2002). An underestimation of their mental health difficulties, however, could lead to neglect of their psychological needs.

What then is a realistic evaluation of the mental health consequences of exposure to mass violence and displacement among refugees? Almost all systematic studies attempting to assess categories such as PTSD and depression across diverse cultural settings have shown rates of these disorders that far exceed those found in nonwar-affected communities of the West (Creamer, Burgess, & McFarlane, 2001; de Jong et al., 2001; Lopes Cardozo et al., 2000; Mollica et al., 1998). Prevalence rates of PTSD yielded by these and other epidemiological studies undertaken in refugee and postconflict settings have varied between 15 and 47% (with one unusual study undertaken in Sierra Leone claiming a rate of 99%) (de Jong, Mulhern, Ford, van der Kam, & Kleber, 2000). In contrast, the prevalence of PTSD in countries such as Australia and the United States ranges from 1.3 (Creamer et al., 2001) to 8% (Kessler, 2000). The discrepancy in rates of depression is even greater, with most refugee populations showing prevalence rates many times higher than recorded in civilian populations.

Another robust finding is the dose-response relationship of trauma to PTSD. Almost all studies, irrespective of their cultural settings or contexts (whether population- or clinic-based), have shown a clear relationship between levels of trauma exposure and risk of PTSD (Mollica et al., 1998; Silove, Sinnerbrink, Field, Manicavasgar, & Steel, 1997). The relationship is both quantitative and qualitative. Overall, the greater number of trauma items endorsed by refugees, the more intense are their symptoms of PTSD (Mollica et al., 1998). At the same time, certain traumas stand out as being particularly pathogenic. For example, recent studies undertaken at multiple sites have confirmed that torture is a particularly threatening form of abuse, resulting in greater levels of psychiatric morbidity (Basoglu, Jaranson, Mollica, & Kastrup, 2001; Shrestha et al., 1998), even when other forms of human rights violations and trauma are taken into account (Silove, Steel, McGorry, Miles, & Drobny, 2002).

Communal Versus Individual Responses

One of the key criticisms leveled at the contemporary use of the term "trauma" is that the concept is based on Western notions of individual psychology and ignores communal responses to adversity, an issue of particular importance to traditional, non-Western societies that retain collectivist views of suffering and adaptation (Eyber & Ager, 2002). This tension between clinical and communal constructs of suffering needs to be acknowledged (Silove et al., 1999b), particularly when research methodologies are used that preferentially focus on one or another of these domains. In essence, qualitative studies aimed at understanding communal responses will not readily enumerate individual forms of psychopathology, with the converse being the case when the methods of epidemiology are applied. The complex challenge is to combine differing methodologies of research in order to achieve a more holistic picture of posttraumatic reactions and consequent forms of adaptation at the communal and individual levels.

Core Adaptive Systems

To encompass such an ecosocial perspective, I have proposed a framework that identifies core systems of adaptation that are disrupted by mass violence and other forms of humanitarian crises (Silove, 1999b). These adaptive systems, it is hypothesized, are represented in the intrapsychic life of individuals as well as in the institutions and practices of the society as a whole. The core systems include safety and security; the maintenance of bonds and interpersonal relationships; effective mechanisms for administering justice; the capacity to perform roles and identities; and the ability to express aspirations that confer meaning, whether these be political, ideological, religious, or spiritual.

A broader concept of trauma would include ecosocial events that threaten the viability and integrity of the systems that support these functions at the individual, small group, and society-wide levels: threats to survival and safety; to the integrity of the family and wider networks; to the defense of human rights and recourse to justice; to a sense of identity conferred by work, study, family, and social roles; and to safeguards and institutions that allow expression of religious, spiritual, and political beliefs.

In each society, historical and cultural factors will determine the specific way in which these adaptive systems are expressed, what constitutes a threat to each one, and how the community reacts to repair the adaptive systems after periods of mass conflict and chaos. After periods of upheaval, most individuals and their groups will be proactive in their efforts to reestablish these systems, and the collective initiative taken to achieve sound recovery and development will, in itself, promote mental well-being. The more successful the repair of these broader ecosocial systems is, the fewer will be those who succumb to a state of chronic psychosocial incapacity as a consequence of the traumas they have suffered.

The Trajectory of Posttraumatic Stress Symptoms

Individual psychological responses to trauma need to be considered within this broader framework. Most persons exposed to traumas of any kind will experience stress responses including sleep disturbances, hyperarousal, hypervigilance, and startle reactions. It is assumed that these fight and flight responses are evolutionarily determined adaptive reactions that prepare the survivor to deal with ongoing risk. Some of these normative reactions, such as heightened arousal and avoidance of threat cues, are included in the criteria of diagnostic categories such as acute stress disorder (ASD) and PTSD, creating difficulties in defining distinct boundaries between normal and morbid responses. It is clear from the general trauma literature and from the majority of studies undertaken among refugees, that most survivors overcome these early posttraumatic stress reactions, with only a minority continuing to suffer from symptoms for prolonged periods of time (Silove & Ekblad, 2002). Nevertheless, where these individual reactions persist and lead to ongoing psychosocial disability, then the balance shifts from the normative toward the pathological.

More information is emerging about the course of posttraumatic stress symptoms in refugees, the antecedent experiences and symptom constellations that can increase risk of prolonged disability, and the individual and social factors that can mitigate or exacerbate symptom trajectories over time. Refugees experience a great deal of emotional instability in the first years following exposure to mass violence, human rights violations, and displacement. The majority of epidemiological studies (Modvig et al., 2000; Mollica et al., 1993, 1999) have been undertaken within this time window, that is, in the immediate or intermediate period following exposure to conflict or in refugee camp settings. Under such conditions of ongoing insecurity and transition, it is not surprising that most studies have shown high rates of persisting posttraumatic stress symptoms.

There is a dearth of longitudinal studies, however, that have followed refugees over longer periods. Two studies undertaken among cohorts of Indo-Chinese refugees in North America stand out in that they have undertaken serial mental health assessments over a 10-year period. Studying Hmong refugees resettled in the United States, Westermeyer and colleagues (1989) showed that psychological stress scores improved substantially over 10 years, although symptom levels did not revert to those of the host population. In a larger study of Indochinese refugees followed in Canada, Beiser and Hou (2001) recorded a progressive reduction in psychiatric symptoms at successive time points over a 10-year period. Remarkably, levels of psychiatric distress in this cohort fell to below that of the host population at the final follow-up period.

Our group undertook a retrospective analysis of the course of post-traumatic affective disorder among 1,100 Vietnamese living in the state of New South Wales, Australia (Steel, Silove, Phan, & Bauman, 2002). The epidemiological sampling approach and the diagnostic measure used (the Composite International Diagnostic Instrument) allowed direct comparison with an Australia-wide epidemiological survey of over 10,000 households conducted 2 years earlier (Henderson et al., 2000). In addition, we included a Vietnamese measure of distress derived from indigenous idioms of mental illness and calibrated according to case assignments made by Chinese traditional healers working in the community.

The study showed that trauma-affected Vietnamese were at many times greater risk of affective disturbance in the first few years after migration, but the risk diminished incrementally as time lapsed since exposure to trauma. By 10 years after the trauma, Vietnamese exposed to moderate levels of trauma reverted to the same prevalence of affective disorder as their nontraumatized compatriots. Those with extreme levels of trauma also showed a substantial decrease in affective disturbance over time, but a residual minority remained impaired at 10 years.

Overall, the study painted a more complex but optimistic picture of the trajectory of trauma reactions in refugees resettled in a stable environment. As a whole, after many years of residency in a stable environment, the Vietnamese community was remarkably healthy from a psychiatric perspective. Even the minority who were most severely traumatized largely recovered, leaving a small but important residual group with chronic symptoms.

Vietnamese did not use more or less health services than native Australians, with the former depending for their psychiatric needs more on primary care physicians, mostly Vietnamese-speaking, than on specialist mental health professionals. From a policy perspective, the study is illuminating in that it suggests that the optimal resettlement environment offered to the Vietnamese, a group that was granted permanent residency and access to all public services and education, led to a good outcome in terms of psychosocial adaptation over time.

In contrast, research among contemporary asylum seekers points to a diametrically different outcome in terms of psychosocial adaptation, a pattern that can be attributed to more recently implemented policies of restriction and deprivation imposed on displaced persons (Ichikawa, 1998; Pourgourides, Sashidharam, & Bracken, 1995; Silove et al., 2000). A series of studies undertaken in Australia among asylum seekers living in the community and in detention paints a picture of persisting and disabling posttraumatic stress symptoms in this group (Silove, 2002a; Sultan & O'Sullivan, 2001). Consistent with the wider refugee literature, previous exposure to trauma and persecution consistently predicts risk of PTSD, depression, and other indices of psychosocial impairment in asylum seekers (Silove et al., 1997; Silove, Steel, McGorry, & Mohan, 1998). In addition, however, multivariate analyses have revealed a substantial contribution of postmigration stresses in perpetuating trauma-related symptoms (Steel et al., 1999). Most of these stresses are the direct consequence of restrictive policies applied to asylum seekers: uncertain residency status; threats of forced repatriation; problematic interactions with immigration officers; lack of work permits; inadequate access to health, social services, education, and financial support; and obstacles to reunion with families living in other countries (Steel & Silove, 2001).

Hence, the emerging data support the general inference drawn from the history of refugee flows referred to earlier. Where displaced persons are offered a welcoming environment and the opportunity to participate freely in the host society, most will recover from traumatic stress reactions over time. Where administrative obstacles are placed in their path, stress reactions will be perpetuated and lead to longer-term disability.

Diversity of Outcomes

An issue that requires further clarification, however, is how to identify in the early posttraumatic phase the minority of refugees who are vulnerable to long-term disability. In considering the multiplicity of trajectories of refugee adaptation, it is important to note that PTSD is not the only reaction to trauma experienced by displaced groups. The traumas suffered by refugees are multiple and complex in their meanings (Silove, 1999a), and as a result, elicit a range of adaptive or maladaptive responses. Apart from PTSD, refugees can manifest symptoms of depression, anxiety, somatization, drug and alcohol abuse, attacks of anger, and a range of maladaptive changes in social behaviors.

The results of a study of Bosnian refugees resettled in Australia (Momartin, Silove, Manicavasager, & Steel, in press) has shown distinctive psychological reaction patterns to specific domains of trauma and stress. Life threat was uniquely associated with risk of PTSD (Momartin et al., 2003), whereas traumatic loss of close family was specifically linked to complicated grief and depression (Momartin et al., in press). Which patterns of response signal a risk of long-term disability? Although there is ample evidence that PTSD is associated with heightened levels of social dysfunction in Western societies, comparable evidence from refugee populations is relatively scarce. Recently, however, Mollica and colleagues (2001) have shown that comorbid PTSD and depression, a common clinical presentation, is particularly disabling in Bosnian refugees, with rates of psychosocial dysfunction in the comorbid group being five times greater than among psychiatrically normal compatriots. That study was undertaken in a refugee camp in the immediate aftermath of the Bosnian war, making it important to examine whether comorbidity is associated with longer-term disability once refugees are repatriated or resettled.

Our group (Momartin et al., in press) found the identical pattern of comorbidity in Bosnian refugees resettled for an average of 5 years in Sydney, Australia, with comorbid PTSD and depression showing higher levels of disability than PTSD alone. The comorbid or high-risk group comprised those exposed to the combined traumas of life threat and traumatic loss. This observation suggests that certain types of complex trauma can leave long-lasting traces on the mental health and psychosocial adaptation of survivors. Among Bosnians, for example, it was common for survivors to report being threatened with death while forced to witness the brutal murder of family members, an experience that is likely to provoke longstanding survivor guilt and self-recrimination. By defining more clearly links between types of trauma, the cultural, cognitive, and social mechanisms that mediate these experiences, and the ongoing influence of the posttraumatic environment, it might become possible to intervene early on a selective basis with the minority of refugees at greatest risk for persisting psychosocial disability.

PRINCIPLES GUIDING PSYCHOSOCIAL INTERVENTIONS

The great variability in the context in which asylum seekers and refugees find themselves and the wide range of psychosocial responses they show, make it imperative to analyze each group and its ecosocial setting in detail in order to tailor interventions to meet specific needs. As indicated, by far the majority of displaced persons are located within low-income countries, and these populations face a range of challenges that differ substantially from the minority who reach developed countries of the West. Hence, there can be specific service provisions that are relevant to some refugee groups but not others, even though common principles of recovery and development underpin all interventions.

As indicated, even in the most threatening humanitarian emergency, communities will make strenuous efforts to reestablish the five ecosocial adaptive systems referred to earlier, that together restore coherence to the collective. Humanitarian interventions should aim to facilitate these self-restorative tendencies (Silove, 1999c). Such programs, if they are effective, provide strategic protection for the most vulnerable by offering life sustaining support (food, water, shelter, medical care); creating mechanisms to reunite families and kinship groups; restoring systems of justice; encouraging the establishment of new roles (work, leadership, training); and assisting in establishing institutions that allow expression of political, social, spiritual, and religious meanings that provide a sense of coherence. How these initiatives are pursued will depend on the resources, context, culture, and historical background of the affected society; but fundamental to the process is the promotion of decision-making and democratic mechanisms in the indigenous community itself, in order to facilitate progress toward self-reliance, dignity, and autonomy.

Mental health professionals do not lead these larger-scale humanitarian programs, but can contribute to them by providing advice and consultancy to policymakers, planners, and program leaders. Where appropriate, specific and carefully designed psychosocial projects led by mental health personnel can be strategic in advancing the larger processes of social recovery. For example, in societies where traditional grieving practices have been disrupted, psychological advice might be sought to restore culturally appropriate rituals and ceremonies. Psychological assistance can also be sought to support witnesses in war crimes tribunals and those participating in truth and reconciliation processes. Multidisciplinary approaches with mental health input will be needed to assist vulnerable groups such as single mothers, unaccompanied minors, and the elderly.

In all instances, mental health contributions to these broader processes should be pursued with pragmatism and constraint, given the limited evidence-base available to guide such work. In particular, practitioners should eschew excessive claims about the power of psychological interventions to remedy complex problems such as intergroup enmities and social responses to human rights violations. Attention to contextual, cultural, and historical issues is essential in order to engage, build trust, and forge partnerships with local workers who should be encouraged to assume leadership in projects as their capacity to do so is developed. In general, small projects should be favored that have clear and achievable objectives and a sustained and measurable impact on the recovery process, as opposed to ambitious, wide-ranging programs with poorly defined targets and whose effects, as a consequence, are difficult to gauge.

Clinical Programs

The focus of clinical programs for refugees also depends heavily on the context. For example, in the early phases of humanitarian emergencies, the survival of the severely mentally disturbed might require priority attention (Silove et al., 2000). During the upheavals in Central Africa, Cambodia, East Timor, and other regions, the severely mentally ill were at risk of abandonment, violence, or abuse. Reports from mental institutions in Kosovo and Iraq have reinforced the concern that in times of chaos, psychiatric inmates are at risk of gross abuses including rape, assault, and eviction.

The Case of East Timor

Our experience (Zwi & Silove, 2002) in setting up the first community mental health service after the humanitarian emergency in East Timor illustrates the extent and diversity of mental health needs in such settings. Even prior to the mass destruction and displacement of populations that overtook that territory in 1999, facilities to treat the mental ill were nonexistent, and there were no trained mental health professionals available to initiate services after the conflict (Silove, 1999a). For these reasons, our focus in setting up PRADET (Psychosocial Recovery and Development in East Timor) was to give priority to those persons with mental disturbance of any type who were at greatest social risk.

Patients referred in the early period after the emergency often had behaved in violent or chaotic ways, were at risk of abuse or constraint (for example, by being chained to trees), or were unable to care for themselves in environments where survival challenges were extreme (Zwi & Silove, 2002). Hence, the guiding principle underlying treatment services in such acute crisis settings needs to extend beyond questions of diagnoses, exposure to trauma, or special demographic groups, instead focusing on the urgency of survival needs for affected persons and their families. In adopting what we have referred to as a social survival and adaptation model, mental health services can support the overall humanitarian mission by ensuring the protection of a particularly vulnerable group in a manner that promotes their dignity and the capacity of caregivers and family to function under extreme conditions.

Services in Developed Countries

In more stable environments, such as in resettlement countries of the West, clinical programs can focus on more specific subgroups of refugees and asylum seekers, especially when generic mental health services are available to treat core severe mental illness such as psychosis. Even then, however, services continue to face new challenges, especially those created by evolving immigration policies. Assisting authorized refugees who have permanent residency to overcome past trauma, the main focus of services in the past (Cunningham & Silove, 1993), differs substantially from attempting to treat asylum seekers held in detention. Although success has been achieved in treating asylum seekers in the community (Drożdek, 1997), we have found that standard treatments such as cognitive behavioral therapy are not effective under conditions of harsh and prolonged detention unless issues of justice and existential despair are confronted. Therapists inevitably become advocates, providing supportive documentation to represent refugee claims, while trying in more general ways to shift government policies that adversely impact the mental health of asylum seekers (Silove, 2002b). It is inevitable that asylum seekers will only respond favorably to therapists who adopt an unambiguous position in supporting their rights, an important ethical and practical consideration.

RESEARCH AND EVALUATION

Research in the field of refugee and asylum mental health has burgeoned in recent decades with a range of epidemiological and risk factor studies being conducted. Nevertheless, researchers in the field face daunting challenges including ethical constraints in studying vulnerable communities, questions from professionals in the field about the legitimacy of Western-derived research methods and measures (Summerfield, 1999), and general neglect by health professionals of the epidemic nature of torture and other human rights abuses (Silove, 2003).

Yet research and evaluation are critical to a field in which there is a dearth of studies attesting to the effectiveness of interventions, whether psychosocial, clinical, or communal. Without a firm evidence base, all elements of work will be impeded, and the authority with which mental health professionals can advocate for changes in policy and the development of services will be weakened. Quantitative and qualitative methods each have a place, making it important to foster frameworks of interdisciplinary inquiry that acknowledge the value of a multiplicity of methods and perspectives. Unless there is greater convergence in existing epistemologies and research approaches, the field will remain prey to radical oscillations in the messages it portrays, with assertions being based more on limited perspectives and preconceptions than on comprehensive empirical data. The recent controversy about the relevance of trauma to refugees is a striking example of such polarizations. Clearly, resolution of the debate will not be brought about by further argument, but by advances in knowledge that are empirically grounded.

CONCLUSIONS

This chapter has highlighted the key issues that continue to challenge professionals working in the fields of asylum and refugee mental health. Advocating for this group has become even more pressing given the converging forces of increased mass displacement, the contemporary retreat by some world leaders on human rights, and a preoccupation with global security rather than with humanitarian responsibility.

Recent policies of deterrence, in particular, represent a new threat to the psychosocial well-being of asylum seekers. In addition, polarizations among professionals in representing theoretical understandings can confuse policymakers and inadvertently encourage neglect of the mental health needs of refugees. As a consequence, the pressure is increasing for mental health advocates to muster sound empirical data to support advocacy and effective interventions for refugees. A major challenge is to formulate and evaluate models of treatment that deal not only with the impact of past trauma on current functioning, but that focus on the capacity of displaced persons to confront immediate insecurities and future threats. The need for such a shift in therapeutic orientation is an indictment of contemporary public policy, illustrating how political decision-making itself can generate global public health problems. In that respect, there can be no respite for mental health professionals in their efforts to safeguard the psychological well-being of displaced persons. Fortunately, the unbroken spirit of refugees provides the motivation needed by their helpers to continue the struggle.

REFERENCES

Amnesty International. (2002). *Amnesty International report 2002*. London: Amnesty International Publications.

Basoglu, M., Jaranson, J., Mollica, R., & Kastrup, M. (2001). Torture and mental health: A researcher overview. In E. Gerrity, T. Keane, & F. Tuma (Eds.), *The mental health consequences of torture* (pp. 35–65). New York: Plenum Press.

Beiser, M., & Hou, F. (2001). Language acquisition, unemployment, and depressive disorder among Southeast Asian refugees: a 10-year study. *Social Science & Medicine, 53*, 1321–1334.

Bunce, C. (1997). Doctors complain about treatment of asylum seekers in Britain. *British Medical Journal, 314*, 393.

Courtland Robinson, W. (1998). *Terms of Refuge — The Indochinese exodus and the international response*. London, England: Zed Books.

Creamer, M., Burgess, P., & McFarlane, A. C., (2001). Posttraumatic stress disorder: Findings from the Australian National Survey of Mental Health and Well-being. *Psychological Medicine, 31*, 1237–1247.

Cunningham, M., & Silove, D. (Eds.). (1993). *Principles of treatment and service development for refugee survivors of torture and trauma*. New York: Plenum Press.

de Jong, J. T., Komproe, I. H., van Ommeren, M., El Masri, M., Araya, M., Khaled, N., et al. (2001). Lifetime events and posttraumatic stress disorder in 4 postconflict settings. *JAMA, 286*(5), 555–562.

de Jong, K., Mulhern, M., Ford, N., van der Kam, S., & Kleber, R. (2000). The trauma of war in Sierra Leone. *Lancet, 355*(9220), 2067–2068.

Drožđek, B. (1997). Follow-up study of concentration camp survivors from Bosnia-Herzegovina: Three years later. *Journal of Nervous & Mental Disease, 185*(11), 690–694.

Eyber, C., & Ager, A. (2002). Conselho: Psychological healing in displaced communities in Angola. *Lancet, 360*(9336), 871.

Henderson, S., Andrews, G., & Hall W. (2000). Australia's mental health: An overview of the general population survey. *Australian & New Zealand Journal of Psychiatry, 34*, 197–205.

Herlihy, J., Scragg, P., & Turner, S. (2002, February 9). Discrepancies in autobiographical memories — implications for the assessment of asylum seekers: Repeated interviews study. *British Medical Journal, 324*, 324–327.

Ichikawa, M. (1998). *Trauma exposure, post-migration stressors and psychiatric disorders among Burmese asylum seekers in Japan.* Cardiff, England: University of Wales College of Medicine.

Kessler, R. C. (2000). Posttraumatic stress disorder: The burden to the individual and to society. *Journal of Clinical Psychiatry, 61*(5), 4–12.

Lopes Cardozo, B., Vergara, A., Agani, F., & Gotway, C. A. (2000). Mental health, social functioning, and attitudes of Kosovar Albanians following the war in Kosovo. *JAMA, 284*(5), 569–577.

Modvig, J., Pagaduan-Lopez, J., Rodenburg, J., Salud, C. M., Cabigon, R. V., & Panelo, C. I. (2000). Torture and trauma in post-conflict East Timor. *Lancet, 356*(9243), 1763.

Mollica, R. F., Donelan, K., Tor, S., Lavelle, J., Elias, C., Frankel, M., et al. (1993). The effect of trauma and confinement on functional health and mental health status of Cambodians living in Thailand-Cambodia border camps. *JAMA, 270*(5), 581–586.

Mollica, R. F., McInnes, K., Pham, T., Smith Fawzi, M. C., Murphy, E., & Lin, L. (1998). The dose-effect relationships between torture and psychiatric symptoms in Vietnamese ex-political detainees and a comparison group. *Journal of Nervous & Mental Disease, 186*(9), 543–553.

Mollica, R. F., McInnes, K., Sarajlic, N., Lavelle, J., Sarajlic, I., & Massagli, M. P. (1999). Disability associated with psychiatric comorbidity and health status in Bosnian refugees living in Croatia. *JAMA, 282*(5), 433–439.

Mollica, R. F., Sarajlic, N., Chernoff, M., Lavelle, J., Vukovic, I. S., & Massagli, M. P. (2001). Longitudinal study of psychiatric symptoms, disability, mortality, and emigration among Bosnian refugees. *JAMA, 286*, 546–554.

Momartin, S., Silove, D., Manicavasagar, V., & Steel, Z. (2003). Dimensions of trauma associated with PTSD caseness, severity and functional impairment: A study of Bosnian Muslim refugees resettled in Australia. *Journal of Social Science & Medicine, 57*(5), 775–781.

Momartin, S., Silove, D., Manicavasagar, V., & Steel, Z. (in press). Comorbidity of PTSD and depression: Associations with trauma exposure, symptoms severity and functional impairment in Bosnian refugees. *Journal of Affective Disorders.*

Pourgourides, C., Sashidharan S. P., & Bracken, P. (1995). *A second exile: The mental health implications of detention of asylum seekers in the United Kingdom.* Birmingham, England: North Birmingham Mental Health NHS Trust.

Shrestha, N. M., Sharma, B., van Ommeren, M., Regmi, S., Makaju, R., Komproe, I. et al. (1998). Impact of torture on refugees displaced within the developing world: Symptomatology among Bhutanese refugees in Nepal. *JAMA, 280*(5), 443–448.

Silove, D. (1999a). Health and human rights of the East Timorese. *Lancet, 353*(12), 2067.

Silove, D. (1999b). The psychosocial effects of torture, mass human rights violations and refugee trauma: Towards and integrated conceptual framework. *Journal of Nervous & Mental Disease, 187,* 200–207.

Silove, D. (1999c). The psychosocial effects of torture, mass human rights violations, and refugee trauma: Toward an integrated conceptual framework. *Journal of Nervous & Mental Disease, 187*(4), 200–207.

Silove, D. (2002a). The asylum debacle in Australia: A challenge for psychiatry. *Australian & New Zealand Journal of Psychiatry, 36*(3), 290–296.

Silove, D. (2002b). Conflict in East Timor: Genocide or expansionist occupation. *Human Rights Review, 1,* 62–79.

Silove, D. (2003, May 3). Overcoming obstacles in confronting torture. *Lancet, 361,* 1555.

Silove, D., & Ekblad, S. (2002). How well do refugees adapt after resettlement in Western countries? *Acta Psychiatrica Scandinavica, 106*(6), 401–402.

Silove, D., Ekblad, S., & Mollica, R. (2000). The rights of the severely mentally ill in post-conflict societies. *Lancet, 355*(9214), 1548–1549.

Silove, D., Sinnerbrink, I., Field, A., Manicavasagar, V., & Steel, Z. (1997). Anxiety, depression and PTSD in asylum-seekers: Associations with pre-migration trauma and post-migration stressors. *British Journal of Psychiatry, 170,* 351–357.

Silove, D., Steel, Z., McGorry, P., Miles, V., & Drobny, J. (2002). The impact of torture on post-traumatic stress symptoms in war-affected Tamil refugees and immigrants. *Comprehensive Psychiatry, 43*(1), 49–55.

Silove, D., Steel, Z., McGorry, P., & Mohan, P. (1998). Trauma exposure, post-migration stressors, and symptoms of anxiety, depression and post-traumatic stress in Tamil asylum-seekers: Comparison with refugees and immigrants. *Acta Psychiatrica Scandinavica, 97*(3), 175–181.

Steel, Z., & Silove, D. M. (2001). The mental health implications of detaining asylum seekers. *Medical Journal of Australia, 175,* 596–599.

Steel, Z., Silove, D., Bird, K., McGorry, P., & Mohan, P. (1999). Pathways from war trauma to posttraumatic stress symptoms among Tamil asylum seekers, refugees, and immigrants. *Journal of Traumatic Stress, 12*(3), 421–435.

Steel, Z., Silove, D., Phan, T., & Bauman, A. (2002). The long-term impact of trauma on the mental health of Vietnamese refugees resettled in Australia. *Lancet, 360,* 156–162.

Sultan, A., & O'Sullivan, K. (2001). Psychological disturbances in asylum seekers held in long-term detention: a participant–observer account. *Medical Journal of Australia, 175,* 593–596.

Summerfield, D. (1999). A critique of seven assumptions behind psychological trauma programmes in war-affected areas. *Social Science & Medicine, 48*(10), 1449–1462.

Summerfield, D. (2003). Fighting "terrorism" with torture. *British Medical Journal, 326,* 773–774.

United Nations High Commissioner for Refugees (2001). *The State of the World's Refugees: A Humanitarian Agenda.* New York: Oxford University Press.

U.S. Committee for Refugees (2003). World Refugee Survey. Retrieved on April 16, 2004 from http/www.refugees.org/downloads/wrs03/55keyStatistics.pdf.

Watters, C. (1998). *The mental health needs of refugees and asylum seekers: Key issues in research and service development.* London, England: Avebury.

Westermeyer, J., Neider, J., & Callies, A. (1989). Psychosocial adjustment of Hnong refugees during their first decade in the United States: A longitudinal study. *Journal of Nervous & Mental Disease, 177,* 132–139.

Zwi, A., & Silove, D. (2002). Hearing the voices — mental health services in East Timor. *Lancet, 360*(Suppl. 1), 45–46.

3

A Global Perspective of Torture, Political Violence, and Health

JENS MODVIG AND JAMES M. JARANSON

INTRODUCTION

Torture, political repression, and armed conflict pose an immense threat to individuals and populations on numerous levels. Whether the violence is targeted toward the individual (as in torture) or toward a whole population (as in war), the potential of death or injury of those subjected to such violence is evident. When such threats lead to escape, internal displacement, or asylum seeking in a different country, an additional number of threats are added, including a possible cumulative or synergetic impact on the victim's health, function, and well-being.

This chapter will (a) review political violence and torture, including the atrocities, global occurrence, and impact on the health of individuals and populations; (b) discuss definitions of torture and organized violence; (c) provide a broad account of types of violence; (d) present briefly the current knowledge regarding interactions between threats and their biopsychosocial response mechanisms; and (e) review available data about torture and post-traumatic stress prevalence among victims of torture and related human rights violations. Working definitions of some of the key concepts used in this chapter are presented in Table 3.1.

TABLE 3.1   Definition of Key Concepts

Harm	Pain, suffering, loss, injury, or death
Danger	A situation characterized by increased risk of harm
Threat	A phenomenon (statement or situation) with an inherent potential of harm
Stressor	A stimulus that produces a stress-response
Traumatic event	An event that produces fear, helplessness, or horror
Violence	Intentional use of force or power, which is likely to produce harm to the one(s) subjected to violence
Political violence	Violence committed by groups driven by attempts to change or resist change to a country's political system
Pain	A discomforting sensation manifesting a threat to the physical integrity
Suffering	A discomforting sensation manifesting a threat to the physical and/or the psychological integrity (also includes distress — "mental pain")
Health	The potential of a long life in well-being

TORTURE AND POLITICAL VIOLENCE

The Concept of Torture

Definitions of torture have been formulated by Amnesty International, the United Nations, the World Medical Association (Gurr & Quiroga, 2001), as well as by several regional and national instruments (International Rehabilitation Council for Torture Victims, 2001). General features of the definitions are deliberate infliction of pain for a specific purpose; whereas characteristics of the pain (e.g., severe pain or suffering, either physical or mental) and the perpetrator (a person representing the government or a non-state actor) differ.

In the U.N. Convention Against Torture and Other Cruel, Inhuman or Degrading Treatment or Punishment (United Nations, 1984), an important exception is given, that is, pain and suffering inherent in lawful sanctions. Thus, the United Nations excludes lawful punishments such as amputation, stoning, and flogging from classification as torture. However, these punishments still involve severe pain inflicted intentionally for a specific purpose by a representative of the state and therefore can be labeled "legalized torture."

Related human rights violations include the concept of "other cruel, inhuman or degrading treatment," often referred to as "ill-treatment." These include acts or conditions that, with regard to the severity of pain, the presence of specific purpose, or the intentional infliction, do not amount to torture. Jurisprudence of international and regional human rights courts and general comments of the U.N. Committee Against Torture are constantly trying to make the distinction between torture and ill treatment more precise (Ovey & White, 2002).

The practice of torture can be a consciously and selectively used tool in the oppression of political opponents, or torture can reflect the standard method of criminal investigation to obtain confessions and thereby keep law enforcement empowered over the general population. Laws and Iacopino (2002) reported an example of politicized use of torture in their study of police torture in Punjab, India. Interviews with 181 torture victims regarding the reasons for the torture revealed (in decreasing order) that 40% were interrogated for information about militants, 22% were accused of providing resources for militants, 13% were suspected of being militants, and 10% were accused of illegal arms possession.

Political Violence

Violence is, according to the World Health Organization, the intentional, actual, or threatened use of physical force or power, resulting in, or with a high likelihood of, injury (adapted from Krug, Dahlberg, Mercy, Zwi, & Lozano, 2002). It can be directed against individuals (self-directed or interpersonal), groups, or communities, and committed by individuals or groups (collective violence). The nature of the violence can be physical, sexual, psychological, or involve neglect or deprivation. The motives for the use of collective violence can be social, political, or economic (Krug, Dahlberg, Mercy, Zwi, & Lozano, 2002, p. 6).

Thus, collective violence is defined as "the instrumental use of violence by ... members of a group ... against another group ... in order to achieve political, economic or social objectives (Krug, Dahlberg, Mercy, Zwi, & Lozano, 2002, p. 215). Collective violence can comprise war, terrorism, and other political conflicts, state-perpetrated violence (genocide, repression, disappearances, and torture), and the violence of organized crime.

Political violence comprises the subset of collective violence, which is driven by political motives, or "attempts to change or resist change to a country's political system or aspects of it" (Pinto & Wardlaw, 1989), as opposed to violence driven by social or economic motives.

However, attention has been drawn to the phenomenon of competing "labels," which describes events and groups, particularly in the public rhetoric of various political interest groups (Simpson & Rauch, 1993). This often results in a contest of who is more responsible for the escalating political violence. In addition, a further complicating factor discussed by the same authors is the dual dynamic of the criminalization of political violence and the politicization of crime. Thus, political objectives can rally social and economic subobjectives and lead to alliances between groups, each of which is pursuing political, social, or economic motives.

Most societies accept the use of violence by law enforcement (e.g., police, prison staff, military, intelligence, and security agencies) on behalf of the society within legally defined limits as necessary to control antisocial behavior (rule of law). In democratic societies, where governments are accountable to civil society, laws regulate the use of violence, and citizens have a right to complain when laws are allegedly broken. Citizens in a democracy also expect access to an impartial, credible, prompt, and competent investigation of any case of violence to assess whether it was in the public's best interest. Governments' accountability to civil society in the areas of public use of violence and public processing of abuse complaints is of key concern, and it is often a litmus test of true democracy and compliance with internationally agreed upon standards for civil and political rights.

In the special case of torture and other cruel, inhuman, or degrading treatment, the U.N. Convention Against Torture (United Nations, 1984) and the Istanbul Protocol and Principles (Allden et al., 2001) set the internationally agreed-upon standards. These include, inter alia, that there is an absolute prohibition against the use of torture and that an independent expert body shall investigate all allegations of torture impartially and promptly.

A second area of concern is the public management of nongovernmental use of violence and of public initiatives to control such violence. Failure to implement effective measures toward such violence can indicate bad-will, reflecting that social and economically motivated violence might serve a political purpose, as explained above.

Individual Appraisal of Acts of Political Violence

Violence, political or other, can produce direct physical injuries or even death. In addition, however, violence constitutes a threat to the potential for future well-being, that is, a threat to health. Use of physical force, including pain, represents a threat to the biological integrity, and use of psychological force represents a threat to the integrity of the self (cf. Chapman & Gavrin, 1999).

Such threats represent danger and constitute high-level stressors that challenge a current life situation's homeostasis, ranging from deferred fulfillment of needs to death. Silove (1999) proposes that torture and related abuses can challenge five core adaptive systems: ensuring safety, attachment, justice, identity-role, and existential-meaning (see also Chapter 23 in this volume). This conceptual framework can facilitate further research into exactly how the individual appraisal of violence can modify the relationship between the threat and its health impact.

In analyzing the impact of threats originating from political violence on health, characteristics of the threat, such as intensity and duration, or whether the threat applies to that particular individual or to a larger group, can have an important impact on the individual. For example, short-term and long-term exposure to stressors produces, respectively, acute and chronic biological stress reactions, which have differing impacts on the immune system and the brain plasticity (McEwen, 2000b). An implicit feature of acuteness and chronicity is the intensity of the stressor: an acute stressor (*an event*) is of high intensity and short duration, for example, an urgent life-threat; and a chronic stressor (*a condition*) is of lower intensity and longer duration, for example, deprivation of needs during detention.

Further, the degree of targeting individuals versus groups or populations likely influences the individual's appraisal of the threat. In torture, the extreme life threat is targeted toward that particular individual. In ethnic cleansing, where a village is emptied by means of burning houses, threats, and killings, the target is a village population representing a subset of an entire ethnic population. In retrospective cognitive processing of the violent event, the challenge is not only to understand why the perpetrating group used violence against others, but also why the individual was singled out.

There can be other relevant categories than those addressed, such as a series of repetitive acute extreme stressors or paraindividual targeting (e.g., witnessing violence targeted toward other individuals because of characteristics that apply to oneself, as well).

Differences of significance to the impact of political violence can be found in the dimensions of individual targeting and the duration and intensity of the stressor (Schnurr, Friedman, & Bernardy, 2002). The degree of life threat, that is, the assessed risk of surviving the event, can be a key dimension to understanding the impact of political violence. Thus, the acute, individually targeted threat is more likely to represent imminent death than the chronic, population-targeted stressor. In addition, the collective threat can comprise a potentially consoling factor through the shared destiny, such as, solidarity, identity, and mutual support. Table 3.2 provides examples of political violence, divided by acute-chronic characteristics and whether the violence is directed toward an individual, a group, or a population.

Obviously, the individual assessment of and reaction to the violent event or condition is of paramount significance for the appraisal, for example, the assessment of inherent life danger. Cumulative life experiences are an important component here. Some findings indicate that the psychological preparedness for torture through previous political activity can have protective significance for its mental health impact (Basoglu et al., 1997). In contrast, a history of traumatic events seems to increase the vulnerability toward new traumatic events (Solomon & Prager, 1992).

TABLE 3.2 Categories of Political Violence by Duration/Intensity and Target Level

	Target: Individual	Target: Group	Target: Population
Event or Acute Stressor (occurs in seconds, minutes, hours, or days)	An individual subjected to torture for hours during detention or experiencing the killing of a relative	A village population forced to abandon the village because houses are burned and killings are threatened	A population targeted in a war/combat situation
Condition or Chronic Stressor (occurs in weeks, months, or years)	Solitary confinement for months, or waiting a lengthy period for an asylum application to be processed	Imprisonment under harsh conditions	A population subjected to discrimination, poverty, famine, and suppression

The Biopsychosocial Response to Danger

According to the theory of stressor and stress response as presented by Selye (1976), a stressor evokes a generalized stress response that sets the organism in a state of physiological and mental arousal. The main components have been shown to be the corticotropin-releasing hormone (CRH) and locus ceruleus-norepinephrine/autonomic systems, the pituitary-adrenal axis (PAA), and the limbic system. The stress response is considered useful for survival through adaptation to and/or future avoidance of external threats (Chrousos & Gold, 1992; Tsigos & Chrousos, 2002).

CRH can exert increased arousal and responsiveness to stressful stimuli centrally, independent of the PAA, and can thus be involved in activating the central nervous system in response to environmental threats. This part of the stress response can be particularly sensitive to overload (Koob, 1999). The concept of allostatic load (McEwen, 2000a, 2002) reflects the impact of repeated or constant activation of the stress response on the body and brain. Such impact is, for example, nerve cell atrophy of the hippocampus (Bremner et al., 1995), which is considered to have clinical ramifications for conditions like posttraumatic stress disorder (McEwen, 2000a). Other possible allostatic overload indicators are increased CRH in cerebrospinal fluid (Bremner et al., 1997) and low urine cortisol (Yehuda et al., 1995).

Of particular interest to the relationship between stressors and their long-term health impact is the memory encoding in amygdala of sensory stimuli associated with the danger, which seems to be facilitated by the adrenergic stress response (Charney, Deutch, Krystal, Southwick, &

Davis, 1993; Gurr & Quiroga, 2001; Southwick et al., 2002). This implies that the more extreme the perception of danger, the stronger the memory encoding, and, presumably, the more severe and prolonged the impact on the individual. This results in avoidance, intrusion, and hyperarousal.

This overload of the stress-response system corresponds to the concept of posttraumatic stress, induced by traumatic events that are able to create a state of fear, hopelessness, or horror in response to the threat of injury or death (Yehuda, 2002).

The individual's behavioral, emotional, and cognitive coping with the stressor, as well as the individual's appraisal of the stressor, can further modify the resulting impact on health and function (Lazarus & Folkman, 1984). This was empirically supported in a study of former political prisoners from Palestine (Kanninen, Punamäki, & Qouta, 2002).

THE OCCURRENCE OF TORTURE

Obtaining Information about Events of Torture

Torture is often clandestine and surrounded by silence for several reasons. The perpetrators (those who commit torture directly, those who order it, and those who are administratively and politically responsible for it) seek to hide the fact that the torture took place. The survivor of torture frequently carries the burden of feelings of guilt and shame, which makes it too painful and humiliating to tell the outside world about the torture. Torture methods are described in Table 3.3.

The factual information of the torture event (who did what to whom, how, when, where, and why) can almost only be obtained from the torture survivor, who might need treatment and support. For human and ethical reasons, the gathering of information can best be obtained in a supportive environment with facilities to provide treatment. Even in such a supportive environment, the emotional barriers often prevent the full accounting of the atrocities until a long-term confidential relationship with the therapist has been established. This silence makes it particularly difficult to provide data on torture occurrence; whereas this does not apply to the same degree to exposure to other types of political violence.

THE PSYCHOLOGY OF PERPETRATORS

Understanding the phenomenon of torture includes the puzzling question of what makes torturers torture others? What factors permit law enforcement personnel to be ordered to inflict horrifying acts of pain and suffering on other people? Are they hardened, evil, and sadistic psychopaths with no conscience? Or do the setting and framework

TABLE 3.3 Overview of Torture Methods

Physical Methods	Psychological Methods
Blunt Trauma	Humiliation
Unsystematic (beatings all over)	Verbal humiliations (e.g., sexual
Systematic (e.g., under the soles	humiliations and mocking)
of the feet, i.e., falanga; on both	Forced humiliating actions (e.g.,
ears, i.e., telephono)	breaking taboos, renouncing
Penetrating Trauma	ideological, political, or religious
Stinging (e.g., under nails)	foundation)
Cuttings (mutilation)	Depersonalization/dehumanization
Amputations	(e.g., being called by number
Shots	instead of name, blindfolded for
Crushing Trauma	weeks or months)
Mutilation of (e.g., extremities by	Interrogation in the nude
trampling)	Threats
Positional Torture	Against the victim (e.g., death
Fixation/restriction of movement	threats, threats of rape, torture)
by use of ropes, chains, straps	Against the victims family
Fixation in forced unphysiological	Mock Executions
positions, (e.g., in small boxes,	Deprivation
rooms, or cages [the tortoise])	Of light and sound
Suspension with arms tied behind	Of food and drink
the back (palestinian hanging), on	Of access to toilet facilities
a stick in the hollows of the knees,	Of sleep
locked with tied wrists (the parrot	Of company
stick), in feet or hair	Of access to medicine and medical
Shaking	assistance
Shaking of the head for a long time	Experiencing the Torture of Others
Asphyxiation	
Near-drowning (e.g., in polluted	
water [submarino])	
Near-suffocation (e.g., by use of	
ropes or plastic bags [dry	
submarino])	
Chemical and Physical Torture	
Chemical tissue damage (e.g., skin,	
mucous membranes, underlying	
tissue) by use of acids, bases,	
inhalation of chili powder,	
kerosene, etc.	
Physical tissue damage by use of	
electricity, cold, heat, or fire (burns)	

TABLE 3.3 *Continued*

Physical Methods	Psychological Methods
Pharmacological and Microbiological Torture	
Forced intake of toxic doses of (e.g., neuroleptics)	
Inoculation of pathogenic bacteria or viruses (e.g., HIV)	
Deprivation of access to necessary medicine (e.g., insulin)	
Sexual Torture	
Rape, possibly forced between two victims	
Instrumentation of genitals	
Animal Torture	
Enticing animals (dogs, rats, insects, etc.) to assault or attack a fixated victim	

of torture facilitate the practice of torture independent of major personality-related proneness?

Several studies have supported the plausibility of the latter explanation. Through social learning, systems of reward and punishment, propaganda, comradeship, and so forth, learned obedience to the authority can explain the behavior of torturers (Crelinsten & Schmid, 1993; Gibson, 1991; Haritos-Fatouros, 1988). According to this explanation, anybody prone to social learning could become a torturer when subjected to the appropriate environment.

An in-depth interview study of 21 Greek military policemen serving during the 1967–1974 Greek military dictatorship was recently published (Haritos-Fatouros, 2003). Five of these were regular torturers during the dictatorship, while 11 were occasional torturers. The study addressed the systems and processes of selecting, creating, and using torturers as applied by the Special Interrogation Section (EAT) of the military police. The study also addressed the personality history of the torturers.

The criteria that were applied for the selection of torturer trainees included conservative family beliefs, rural background, intelligence, education, obedience, toughness, good performance in group beatings, discretion, and trustworthiness. After selection, the candidates were subjected to a transformation process involving training programs for the torture chambers, propaganda against "inner enemies," and model learning. In addition, the system provided for advanced training to create chief torturers, who had the competence of practicing individual torture without supervision.

The case studies of these torturers showed stories of ordinary men raised in poor semiurban or rural Greek environments, but with little evidence of childhood abuse or sadistic psychopathology. In conclusion, the creation of torturers is a conscious and systematic process by systems, not individual occurrences by extreme personalities.

Torture Occurrence on the Global Level

The available data on global torture occurrence are provided, inter alia, by human rights organizations (Amnesty International, 2001; Human Rights Watch, 2003), by the United Nations (e.g., United Nations, 2002), and by the U.S. Department of State (2002) in their yearly human rights reports. The data are provided through reports of single cases of torture, which allow very crude estimations of torture occurrence on the country level. The available level of information is thus far from a systematic coverage of torture occurrence.

The International Rehabilitation Council for Torture Victims (IRCT) has made a global analysis of torture occurrence based on all four sources (IRCT, 2001). The results of the analysis showed that torture and ill-treatment are consistently reported as widespread by all four sources in 32 countries. Torture and ill-treatment are reported to be widespread by at least one of the sources or to occur sporadically by at least two sources in a total of 80 countries. It is reasonable to assume that, in a quarter of the world's countries, torture is practiced systematically, and that in more than half of the countries, torture occurs on a regular basis.

Global estimates of the prevalence of tortured victims remain crude because of a lack of epidemiological data. An approximation can be obtained by estimating the magnitude of particular high-risk groups and the torture prevalence in these groups. Such groups comprise refugees and persons who are or have been under detention.

Studies of Torture Prevalence

Few studies have estimated the prevalence of exposure to torture among detainees. Paker, Paker, and Yüksel (1992) found, in a study of 246 long-term prisoners in one Turkish prison, that 208 (85%) had been tortured. Studies of torture prevalence in refugee populations or even in national surveys are more abundant and summarized in Table 3.4.

Studies of national samples show a prevalence ranging from 8 to 30%, studies in near-area refugee settings from 3 to 16%, and studies in Western refugee settings from 18 to 76% (provided those that witnessed torture were considered torture victims as well). Too many uncertainties are attached to the measurements presented to allow clear general conclusions to be drawn; there are differences in assessment method, selection mechanisms, and composition of the study populations. However, the studies of composite refugee populations in Western settings can share selection mechanisms, and the available estimates are relatively close, based upon large samples. In conclusion, 10 to 30% of refugees in Western settings are torture victims.

Studies of Torture's Impact on Individuals

Posttraumatic stress disorder (PTSD), together with other anxiety disorders and depression, is the most common mental disorder diagnosed in the aftermath of severely traumatic events (Saraceno, Saxena, & Maulik, 2002). However, despite an increase in knowledge, the prevalence of mental health problems remains unknown. Recent epidemiological evidence indicates that PTSD can be identified across cultures, but it occurs in only a minority of persons exposed to mass conflict, with prevalence rates varying between 9 and 37% (Table 3.5). Prevalence rates of anxiety disorder, including posttraumatic stress and depressive symptoms, have varied by the latency of time and severity of trauma (Mollica, McInnes, Poole, & Tor, 1998). The literature also shows that among refugee populations, social factors such as political asylum (compared with permission to stay on humanitarian grounds), unemployment, loss of meaningful structure and activity in life, inadequate proficiency in the language of host country, conflicts with children, marriage, and Buddhist spirituality have been found to be related to depression or other mental disorders (Saraceno et al., 2002).

Most studies have been undertaken with treatment populations, although large population-based surveys or case-control studies are less common (Table 3.5). De Jong et al. (2001) studied postconflict populations in Algeria, Cambodia, Gaza, and Ethiopia, finding rates of PTSD ranging from 16 to 37%, with rates significantly higher in torture survivors (Table 3.5). Jaranson et al. (2003), using a cut-off PCL-C score of ≥50 (range 17 to 85) to indicate suspected PTSD in a community-based survey of 1,134 East African refugees in Minnesota, found that 25% of those exposed to torture met this criterion, but only 4% of those traumatized in ways other than by torture. Paker et al. (1992) estimated that 208 Turkish prisoners had significantly more PTSD when compared with other prisoners. Basoglu et al. (1994) showed that 55 Turkish tortured prisoners, who were neither refugees nor internally displaced in Turkey, had higher rates of lifetime (33%) and current (18%) PTSD than 55 nontortured controls.

Smaller surveys have also been conducted. Holtz (1998) compared 35 refugee Tibetan nuns and lay students who were tortured in Tibet with controls who were neither imprisoned nor tortured. Torture survivors had significantly higher rates of anxiety (54% vs. 29%) but not depression. Allden et al. (1996), using snowball-sampling methodology of 92 tortured Burmese political dissidents in Thailand, found high rates of PTSD (23%) and depressive symptoms.

Symptom levels tend to be higher in refugee camps than in resettlement populations. Mollica, Poole, and Tor (1998), studying Cambodians

TABLE 3.4 Empirical Studies Including Torture Prevalence Estimates in Selected Population Samples

Primary Author	Setting and Sampling Method	Sample Size	Country of Origin/Study	Torture Prevalence
de Jong et al., 2001	National sample: Random selection from community populations in four countries	653	Algeria	8%
		610	Cambodia	9%
		1,200	Ethiopia	26%
		585	Gaza	15%
Modvig, 2001	National sample: Random population sample	1,033 household representatives	East Timor	30%
Shresta et al., 1998	Near-area refugee setting: Identification of all physically tortured refugees in UNHCR camps in southern Nepal	85,078	Bhutan/Nepal	3%
Iacopino et al., 2001	Near-area refugee setting: Random sample of households in Macedonian and Albanian refugee camps for Kosovars	1,180 household representatives	Kosovo/ Macedonia and Albania	4%
Tang & Fox, 2001	Near-area refugee setting: Random sample of Senegalese refugees in two camps in Gambia (N = 242)	80	Senegal/ Gambia	16%
Montgomery & Foldspang, 1994	Western refugee setting: Consecutive sampling of asylum seekers arriving in refugee reception center	74	Middle East/ Denmark	28%
Hondius et al., 2000	Western refugee setting: Refugees recruited to treatment center by flyers	156, dominated by nonhelp-seeking refugees	Turkey, Iran, Holland	76%

TABLE 3.4 *Continued*

Primary Author	Setting and Sampling Method	Sample Size	Country of Origin/ Study	Torture Prevalence
Ekblad et al., 2002	Western refugee setting: Random selection from airline lists of pre-accepted refugees arriving in Sweden ($N = 2,930$)	402 sampled, 218 participated 98 participated in phase 2 follow-up	Kosovo/Sweden	51%
Thonneau et al., 1990	Western refugee setting: All applicants for refugee status in Quebec, Canada, referred to obligatory medical examination	1,994	Composite/Canada	18%
Lie, 2002	Western refugee setting: All settled refugees in 20 municipalities of Norway May 1994–December 1995	791 invited, 462 contributed data	Composite/ Norway	6% (14% witnessed torture)
Kjersem, 1996	Western refugee setting: All asylum-seekers arriving in Denmark January 1, 1986–June 30, 1988	9,579	Composite/ Denmark	10.1%

TABLE 3.5 Percentage of Traumatized Persons With Posttraumatic Stress (PTS) Diagnosis or Significant Symptoms in Population-Based Surveys or Case-Control Studies ($N > 100$) by Descending Order of Sample Size

Primary Author	Population Sample	Trauma Type	Sample Size	Country of Origin/Study	Prevalence Total Sample (%)	Prevalence Nontortured (%)	Prevalence Tortured (%)
de Jong et al., 2001	Post conflict	Torture & War	1,200	Ethiopia/Ethiopia	16	Lower	LT Higher ($p < .001$)
Jaranson et al., 2004	Resettled Refugees	Torture & War	1,134	Somalia & Ethiopia/US	13	4	25
Shrestha et al., 1998	Refugees in Camp*	Torture & War	1,052	Bhutan/Nepal	9	4	14
Mollica et al., 1993	Refugees in Camp	Torture & War	993	Cambodia/Thailand	33	N/A	N/A
van Ommeren et al., 2001	Refugees in Camp*	Torture & War	810	Bhutan/Nepal	N/A	4(C) 15(LT)	43(C) 74(LT)
de Jong et al., 2001	Post-conflict	Torture & War	653	Algeria/Algeria	37	Lower	LT Higher ($p = .003$)
							LT Higher ($p < .001$)

TABLE 3.5 continued

Primary Author	Population Sample	Trauma Type	Sample Size	Country of Origin/Study	Prevalence Total Sample (%)	Prevalence Nontortured (%)	Prevalence Tortured (%)
							LT Higher ($p < .001$)
							N/A
							0
							18(C) 33(LT)

(C) = Current or within past year; (LT) = Lifetime; * = Case-Control Study; N/A = not available.

in a Thai refugee camp, found that a third had posttraumatic stress and twice that many had depression. Shrestha et al. (1998) found that torture predicted significantly more posttraumatic stress, anxiety, and depressive symptoms comparing 526 Bhutanese torture survivors in a Nepalese refugee camp with matched controls. Van Ommeren et al. (2001) subsequently randomly sampled 418 tortured and 392 nontortured Bhutanese refugees from the same frame and showed that torture survivors had more PTSD (43% vs. 4%), somatoform pain, and dissociative disorders in the past year, as well as more lifetime affective and generalized anxiety disorders.

Research Challenges

The main challenge to research seems to be the establishment of reporting systems and instruments to assess torture in order to provide systematic epidemiological data worldwide. The research will have to rely upon internationally agreed-upon standards and formats for systematic and valid data reporting. The instruments to use in research studies when assessing torture and related traumatic events need attention to allow comparison and even metastudies. Presently, the most widely used instrument is the Harvard Trauma Questionnaire, but the trauma event part of this instrument remains to be validated.

Studies of torture and its mental health consequences have rarely included control groups, have generally had small samples, and cannot address the prevalence of torture survival in communities. Any consequences specifically associated with torture, compared with other traumatic events refugees commonly experience, still need to be identified or the effects quantified (Silove, Steel, McGorry, & Drobny, 2002; Steel, Silove, Bird, McGorry, & Mohan, 1999). The sensitivity of the topic of torture makes it difficult to study, and refugees are challenging groups for research under any circumstances (Basoglu, Jaranson, Mollica, & Kastrup, 2001).

REFERENCES

Allden, K., Baykal, T., Iacopino, V., Kirschner, R., Özkalipci, Ö., Peel, M., et al. (Eds.). (2001). *Istanbul protocol: Manual on the effective investigation and documentation of torture and other cruel, inhuman or degrading treatment or punishment.* Geneva, Switzerland: U.N. Office of the High Commissioner for Human Rights.

Allden, K., Poole, C., Chantavanich, S., Ohmar, K., Aung, N. N., & Mollica, R. (1996). Burmese political dissidents in Thailand: Trauma and survival among young adults in exile. *American Journal of Public Health, 86,* 1561–1569.

Amnesty International. (2002). Amnesty International Report 2002. London: Author.

Basoglu, M., Jaranson, J. M., Mollica, R., & Kastrup, M. (2001). Torture and mental health: A research overview. In E. Gerrity, T. M. Keane, & F. Tuma (Eds.), *The mental health consequences of torture* (pp. 35–62). New York: Kluwer Academic/Plenum Publishers.

Basoglu, M., Mineka, S., Paker, M., Aker, T., Livanou, M., & Gök, S. (1997). Psychological preparedness for trauma as a protective factor in survivors of torture. *Psychological Medicine, 27,* 1421–1433.

Basoglu, M., Paker, M., Paker, Ö., Özmen, E., Marks, I., Incesu, C., et al. (1994). Psychological effects of torture: A comparison of tortured with non-tortured political activists in Turkey. *American Journal of Psychiatry, 151,* 76–81.

Bremner, J. D., Licinio, J., Darnell, A., Krystal, J. H., Owens, M. J., Southwick, S. M., et al. (1997). Elevated CSF corticotropin-releasing factor concentrations in posttraumatic stress disorder. *American Journal of Psychiatry, 154,* 624–629.

Bremner, J. D., Randall, P., Scott, T. M., Bronen, R. A., Seibyl, J. P., Southwick, S. M., et al. (1995). MRI-based measurement of hippocampal volume in patients with combat-related posttraumatic stress disorder. *American Journal of Psychiatry, 152,* 973–981.

Chapman, C. R., & Gavrin, J. (1999). Suffering: The contributions of persistent pain. *Lancet, 353,* 2233–2237.

Charney, D. S., Deutch, A. Y., Krystal, J. H., Southwick, S. M., & Davis, M. (1993). Psycho-biologic mechanisms of posttraumatic stress disorder. *Archives of General Psychiatry, 50,* 295–305.

Chrousos, G. P., & Gold, P. W. (1992). The concepts of stress and stress system disorders: Overview of physical and behavioral homeostasis. *JAMA, 267,* 1244–1252.

Crelinsten, R. D., & Schmid, A. P. (Eds.). (1993). *The politics of pain: Torturers and their masters.* Leiden: Centre for the Study of Social Conflicts.

de Jong, J. T. V. M., Komproe, I. H., van Ommeren, M., El Masri, M., Araya, M., Khaled, N., et al. (2001). Lifetime events and posttraumatic stress disorder in 4 postconflict settings. *JAMA, 286,* 555–562.

Ekblad, S., Prochazka, H., & Roth, G. (2002). Psychological impact of torture: A 3-month follow-up of mass-evacuated Kosovan adults in Sweden. Lessons learned for prevention. *Acta Psychiatrica Scandinavica, 106*(Suppl. 412), 30–36.

Gibson, J. T. (1991). Training people in inflict pain: state terror and social learning. *Journal of Humanistic Psychology, 31*(2), 72–87.

Gurr, R., & Quiroga, J. (2001). Approaches to torture rehabilitation: A desk study covering effects, cost-effectiveness, participation, and sustainability. *Torture, 11*(Suppl. 1), 5–35.

Haritos-Fatouros, M. (1988). The official torturer: A learning model for obedience to the authority of violence. *Journal of Applied Social Psychology, 18*(3), 1107–1120.

Haritos-Fatouros, M. (2003). *The psychological origins of institutionalized torture.* London: Routledge Research International Series in Social Psychology.

Holtz, T. (1998). Refugee trauma versus torture trauma: A retrospective controlled cohort study of Tibetan refugees. *Journal of Nervous and Mental Disease, 186,* 24–34.

Hondius, A. J. K., Willigen, L. H. M., Kleijn, W. C., & Ploeg, H. M. (2000). Health problems among Latin-American and Middle-Eastern refugees in the Netherlands: Relations with violence exposure and ongoing sociopsychological strain. *Journal of Traumatic Stress, 13,* 619–634.

Human Rights Watch. (2003). *Human Rights Watch world report 2002.* New York: Author.

Iacopino, V., Frank, M. W., Bauer, H. M., Keller, A. S., Fink, S. L., Ford, D., et al. (2001). A population-based assessment of human rights abuses committed against ethnic Albanian refugees from Kosovo. *American Journal of Public Health, 91,* 2013–2018.

International Rehabilitation Council for Torture Victims. (2001). *International instruments and mechanisms for the fight against torture* (3rd ed.). Copenhagen, Denmark: Author.

IRCT global overview of torture from secondary sources: A country-by-country survey. International Rehabilitation Council for Torture Victims (2000). Copenhagen, Denmark: Unpublished draft.

Jaranson, J. (1998). The science and politics of rehabilitating torture survivors. In J. Jaranson & M. Popkin (Eds.), *Caring for victims of torture* (pp. 15–40). Washington, DC: American Psychiatric Press.

Jaranson, J. M., Butcher, J. N., Halcon, L., Johnson, D. R., Robertson, C., Savik, K., et al. (2004). Somali and Oromo refugees: Correlates of torture and trauma history. *American Journal of Public Health, 94*(4), 591–598.

Kanninen, K., Punamäki, R.-L., & Qouta, S. (2002). The relation of appraisal, coping efforts, and acuteness of trauma to PTS symptoms among former political prisoners. *Journal of traumatic stress, 15,* 245–253.

Kjersem, H. J. (1996). *Migrationsmedicin i Danmark: Vurdering af nogle migrations-medicinske problemstillinger blandt asylsøgere og flygtninge* [Migration medicine in Denmark: Evaluation of a number of migration medicine problems among asylum seekers and refugees]. Copenhagen, Denmark: Danish Red Cross.

Koob, G. F. (1999). Corticotropin-releasing factor, norepinephrine, and stress. *Biological Psychiatry, 46,* 1167–1180.

Krug, E. G., Dahlberg, L. L., Mercy, J. A., Zwi, A. B., & Lozano, R. (2002). *World report on violence and health.* Geneva, Switzerland: World Health Organization.

Laws, A., & Iacopino, V. (2002). Police torture in Punjab, India: An extended survey. *Health and Human Rights, 6*(1), 195–210.

Lazarus, R. S., & Folkman, S. (1984). *Stress, appraisal, and coping.* New York: Springer.

Lie, B. (2002). A 3-year follow-up study of psychosocial functioning and general symptoms in settled refugees. *Acta Psychiatrica Scandinavica, 106,* 415–425.

McEwen, B. S. (2000a). Allostatis and allostatic load: Implications for neuropsychophar-macology. *Neuropsychopharmacology, 22,* 108–124.

McEwen, B. S. (2000b). The neurobiology of stress: From serendipity to clinical relevance. *Brain Research, 886,* 172–189.

McEwen, B. S. (2002). Sex, stress and the hippocampus: Allostasis, allostatic load and the aging process. *Neurobiology of Aging, 23,* 921–939.

Modvig, J., Pagaduan-Lopez, J., Rodenburg, J., Salud, C. M., Cabigon, R. V., Panelo, C. I. (2001). Torture and trauma in post-conflict East-Timor. *Lancet, 356,* 1763.

Mollica, R. F., McInnes, K., Poole, C., & Tor, S. (1998). Dose-effect relationships of trauma to symptoms of depression and post-traumatic stress disorder among Cambodian survivors of mass violence. *British Journal of Psychiatry, 173*, 482–488.

Mollica, R. F., Poole, C., & Tor, S. (1998). Symptoms, functioning, and health problems in massively traumatized populations: The legacy of Cambodian tragedy. In B. P. Dohrenwend (Ed.), *Adversity, stress, and psychopathology* (pp. 34–51). New York: Oxford University Press.

Mollica, R. F., Sarajlic, N., Chernoff, M., Lavelle, J., Vukovic, I. S., & Massagli, M. P. (2001). Longitudinal study of psychiatric symptoms, disability, mortality, and emigration among Bosnian refugees. *JAMA, 286*, 546–554.

Montgomery, E., & Foldspang, A. (1994). Criterion-related validity of screening for exposuere to torture. *Danish Medical Bulletin, 41*, 588–591.

Ovey, C., & White, R. (2002). *Jacobs and White, the European Convention on Human Rights* (3rd ed., pp. 58–89). Oxford, U.K.: Oxford University Press.

Paker, M., Paker, Ö., & Yüksel, S. (1992). Psychological effects of torture: An empirical study of tortured and non-tortured non-political prisoners. In M. Basoglu (Ed.), *Torture and its consequences: Current treatment approaches* (pp. 73–82). Cambridge, UK: Cambridge University Press.

Pinto, S., & Wardlaw, G. (1989). Political violence. *Violence Today, 9*. Retrieved February 9, 2003, from http://www.aic.gov.au/publications/vt/vt9.html.

Saraceno, B., Saxena, S., & Maulik, P. K. (2002). Mental health problems in refugees. In N. Sartorius, W. Gaebel, J. J. López-Ibor, & M. Maj (Eds.), *Psychiatry in society* (pp. 193–220). New York: John Wiley & Sons, Ltd.

Schnurr, P. P., Friedman, M. J., & Bernardy, N. C. (2002). Research on posttraumatic stress disorder: Epidemiology, pathophysiology, and assessment. *Journal of Clinical Psychology, 58*, 877–889.

Selye, H. (1976). Forty years of stress research: principal remaining problems and misconceptions. *Canadian Medical Association Journal, 115*, 53–56.

Shrestha, N. M., Sharma, B., van Ommeren, M., Regmi, S., Makaju, R., Komproe, I., et al. (1998). Impact of torture on refugees displaced within the developing world: Symptomatology among Bhutanese refugees in Nepal. *JAMA, 280*, 443–448.

Silove, D. (1999). The psychosocial effects of torture, mass human rights violations, and refugee trauma: Toward an integrated conceptual framework. *Journal of Nervous and Mental Disease, 187*, 200–207.

Silove, D., Steel, Z., McGorry, P., & Drobny, J. (2002). The impact of torture on post-traumatic stress symptoms in war-affected Tamil refugees and immigrants. *Comprehensive Psychiatry, 43*, 49 55.

Simpson, G., & Rauch, J. (1993). Political violence: 1991. In N. Boister & K. Ferguson-Brown (Eds.), *Human rights yearbook 1992* (pp. 212–239). Cape Town, South Africa: Oxford University Press.

Solomon, Z., & Prager, E. (1992). Elderly Israeli Holocaust survivors during the Persian Gulf war: A study of psychological distress. *American Journal of Psychiatry, 149*, 1707–1710.

Southwick, S. M., Davis, M., Horner, B., Cahill, L., Morgan, C. A., III, Gold, P. E., et al. (2002). Relationship of enhanced norepinephrine activity during memory consolidation to enhanced long-term memory in humans. *American Journal of Psychiatry, 159*, 1420–1422.

Steel, S., Silove, D., Bird, K., McGorry, P., & Mohan, P. (1999). Pathways from war trauma to posttraumatic stress symptoms among Tamil asylum seekers, refugees, and immigrants. *Journal of Traumatic Stress, 12*, 421–435.

Tang, S. M., & Fox, S. H. (2001). Traumatic experiences and the mental health of Senegalese refugees. *Journal of Nervous and Mental Disease, 189,* 507–512.

Thonneau, P., Gratton, J., & Desrosiers, G. (1990). Health profile of applicants for refugee status (admitted into Quebec between August 1985 and April 1986). *Canadian Journal of Public Health, 81,* 182–186.

Tsigos, C., & Chrousos, G. P. (2002). Hypothalamic-pituitary-adrenal axis, neuroendo-crine factors and stress. *Journal of Psychosomatic Research, 53,* 865–871.

United Nations. (1984). *Convention against torture and other cruel, inhuman or degrading treatment or punishment: Adopted and opened for signature, ratification and accession by General Assembly resolution 39/46 of 10 December 1984.* Geneva, Switzerland: Author.

United Nations. (2002). *Report of the Special Rapporteur, Nigel Rodley, submitted pursuant to Commission on Human Rights resolution 2001/62: addendum: summary of cases transmitted to Governments and replies received.* (E/CN.4/2002/76/Add.1). Geneva, Switzerland: Author.

United States Department of State. (2002). *Country reports on human rights practices for 2001.* Washington, DC: Author.

van Ommeren, M., Jong, J. T., Sharma, B., Komproe, I., Thapa, S. B., & Cardena, E. (2001). Psychiatric disorders among tortured Bhutanese refugees in Nepal. *Archives of General Psychiatry, 58,* 475–482.

Yehuda, R. (2002). Post-traumatic stress disorder. *New England Journal of Medicine, 346,* 108–114.

Yehuda, R., Kahana, B., Binder-Brynes, K., Southwick, S. M., Mason, J. W., & Giller, E. L. (1995). Low urinary cortisol excretion in Holocaust survivors with posttraumatic stress disorder. *American Journal of Psychiatry, 152,* 982–986.

4

Ethnocultural Considerations in the Treatment of Refugees and Asylum Seekers

JORGE AROCHE AND MARIANO J. COELLO

ABOUT REFUGEES AND ASYLUM SEEKERS

Culture is an ever present reality in the work we do as counselors, therapists, and helpers. It is also a construct that has attracted a multitude of definitions and has been the subject of many academic debates. For the purpose of this chapter, we will adopt Marsella's (1988) definition of culture as

> shared learned behaviour that is transmitted from one generation to another to promote individual and group adjustment and adaptation. Culture is presented externally as artefacts, roles, and institutions, and is represented internally as values, beliefs, attitudes, cognitive styles, epistemologies, and conscious patterns. (p. 10)

Inevitably, any interpersonal transaction involves an encounter of cultures. Even between individuals from a similar culture, the shared construction of meaning that takes place in therapy involves a subtle exchange of interpretations of different but hopefully compatible worldviews. Developing enough compatibility for this exchange to take place involves building bridges across language and cultural divides. This is seldom a simple task, although we all do this in a multitude of ways. Even assuming a degree of familiarity with the basic aspects of another culture, as Marsella (1988) points out

> Individual subscription to these shared (cultural) values may vary, as does the authority that the culture has in any individual's life. There-fore, knowledge of an individual's degree of ethno-cultural identity is important for understanding the influence of culture on his or her per-ceptions of the world. (p. 10)

The intricacy of the task increases with the number of cultural groups we work with, and with the number of factors impinging on the degree of ethnocultural identity within those groups. By definition, ref-ugees and asylum seekers are people who have obtained or are seeking protection outside their country of origin (or residence), and have therefore been exposed to cultural dislocation and an array of loss expe-riences, as well as multiple stresses and demands to adapt to life in a dif-ferent setting. Few groups confront health care professionals with as many challenges in terms of ethnocultural considerations as refugees do.

It is a sad indictment of the state of the modern world that refugees and asylum seekers originate from almost every continent and from a vast array of language and ethnic groups (UNHCR, 2000). Refugees have survived multiple traumatic situations, placing them at risk of complex posttraumatic clinical presentations. The challenge facing clini-cians (or those in other helping professions) is that refugees are likely the most diverse and heterogenous client group that health care profes-sionals will encounter. For example, a recent client survey among tor-ture and trauma services in Australia, a country with an active refugee and humanitarian program, identified that clients from 66 nationalities and 51 language groups had been assisted in 1999.

Concentrating on language, nationality, or even ethnicity as the major source of the diversity of refugees, however, does not begin to reflect the complexity of this client group. Refugees are often minorities in their country of origin, either because of their ethnicity, religion, politi-cal beliefs or affiliation, or social group. This in turn requires the clini-cian to encounter and understand subcultures and belief systems that might not be representative of those held by either the population at large of their country of origin, or those from a similar group or affilia-tion not living in a situation of discrimination or persecution.

On the other hand, refugees, in a country such as Australia, are often more representative of the diversity of their country of origin than the migrant population that has been carefully selected according to strict criteria. Diversity is also introduced by the nature of their persecution and trauma history, their refugee experience, as represented by their experiences during the time spent between fleeing their country of origin and obtaining protection in a third country, and their degree of acculturation to the host society.

Adding further to this diversity is legal status. The word "refugee" itself is essentially a legal term, and this dimension of the refugee experience is critical. The legal status of people in need of protection determines their rights, their options, and their prospects, as well as their potential access to permanent protection (Farbey, 2002). In the context of first world countries, for example, people with similar traumatic backgrounds might face markedly different situations that impact on their rehabilitation and healing prospects, depending on whether they are still seeking to prove their claims for protection (asylum seekers), have obtained permanent protection, and therefore residence, or only temporary protection with the ever present threat of future repatriation. These differences affect their access to services, resources, their stability in their present situation, the integrity of their family unit, their state of mind, and ultimately, their healing prospects and future. In some countries (including Australia) recent policies of immigration detention of asylum seekers arriving in the country without lawful documentation have introduced yet another variant in this already complex picture by creating different types of refugees with different rights and access to services according to their legal status.

Acknowledging and being prepared to address this diversity and its complexity is crucial to connecting with the individual, the family, or the community from refugee background as a human being whom we might be able to assist in his or her healing despite the many barriers posed by that person's perceived "alienness."

It is not uncommon to see well-meaning and competent clinicians become confused and disconcerted by the lack of familiar clues and contextual landmarks encountered in working with someone from a radically different culture and worldview. Sometimes the initial efforts to prepare for such encounters can be even more baffling, as in a recent situation we were privy to, where a colleague prepared to interview an Iraqi family by finding out information about Iraqis, only to find that the family he was to see did not see Arabic as their language, was not Muslim, and saw itself as quite uncharacteristic of the "Iraqi nationality." It is precisely in the encounter with refugees, marginalized and forced to flee their countries, that reliance on any broad understandings of cultural and religious beliefs and stereotypes prove most inadequate. The clinician must negotiate a complex world where lives have been turned upside down and often culture is both the cause of this pain as well as the pathway to recovery.

The rest of this chapter attempts to explore these complexities. It is grounded on clinical practice and will provide some hints and guidelines to assist clinicians and those in the helping professions in general overcome the challenges posed by various aspects of this diversity. The practical advice in this chapter is based in the experience of the NSW Service for the Treatment and Rehabilitation of Torture and Trauma

(STARTTS), an organization that has assisted over 10,000 refugees in a clinical setting and many more through community development initiatives, and that currently employs 50 clinicians from 18 different nationalities and ethnic backgrounds. Our experience, which mirrors that of hundreds of colleagues around the world, has shown that ethnocultural and sociopolitical differences need not be unsurmountable barriers provided they are taken into consideration in planning and carrying out clinical and psychosocial interventions to assist traumatized refugees.

Ethnocultural Considerations of the Context of Refugee Trauma

The sociopolitical-cultural context in which trauma occurs is central to how people respond to, comprehend, and recover from trauma (Wilson, 1989). In the case of refugees, the trauma is almost always sustained as part of a political and historical process of conflict, often perceived to be associated with ethnocultural and religious issues, that transcends the individual and his or her life span.

The history of the conflict is shaped, and in turn shapes, worldviews, cultural norms, and constructions of society and other people. There is often a parallel process between the individual's trauma history and the historical line of events defining the conflict or social unrest. These two timelines are connected by the traumatic events experienced, and it is necessary to develop an understanding of these events from the client's perspective as an individual and as a community if one is to work effectively with the client's or community's trauma and grief. Trauma is not a disembodied construct, as suggested by DSM-IV, it is a cultural and historical reality that must be entered into by the clinician.

Conflict divides and polarizes societies (Martin-Baro, 1989), and in this context, the attributes and importance of subcultures and group characteristics are often emphasized and exaggerated, becoming major determinants of people's identity.

Belonging to a particular ethnocultural group in some repressive states or conflict situations is associated with a high likelihood of having been exposed to certain types of traumatic experiences. These can involve long, insidious, and sustained persecution, harassment, and discrimination. They can also involve more violent and catastrophic events perpetrated upon that group or, in many cases and over time, a combination of both.

> The Hazaras have suffered from long-standing discrimination, racism, and violation of their human rights by various other ethnic groups. Figures from Human Rights Watch Report (August 1998) on a massacre of 8,000 Hazaras in the city of Mazara-shif and elsewhere show that they suffered enormously under the Taliban regime. (Mehraby, 2002b, p. 31)

Understanding the conflict and particularly the client's construction of the conflict is essential to understanding who the person is and who he or she was before and during the conflict, how that person was affected by the dynamics of power and oppression, and what meaning these experiences had for that indivudual. These dynamics are also particularly important in determining how people experience and cope with different characteristics of the refugee experience and the recovery environment.

Mehraby (2002b), in the context of a joint STARTTS and school intervention with a group of 14 unaccompanied refugee children from Afghanistan, mainly from the Hazara ethnicity, reports that with the exception of two participants from Tajik background, the rest did not consider themselves Afghans, but Hazara from different parts of the Hazarjate region in Afghanistan. Mehraby, who is an Afghan herself, concludes that their statement about their ethnicity "reflected their loss of identity and belonging as Afghans "(p. 33).

In the case of longstanding conflicts, such as those in Afghanistan, Sri Lanka, Palestine, East Timor, Ethiopia, Rwanda, and Uganda, many refugees might have never experienced a situation of relative peace and security. Younger people might have been born and become adults in a context of continuous war and violence, and their perception of their culture and its symbols can be skewed or filtered by the aspects of that culture that are most relevant to the conflict. In a sense, they could have lived their whole lives under the fog of war or persecution. This fog, however, is likely to have also obscured our (assuming that the counselor/therapist or helper is at least partially representative of the host country society and worldview) knowledge and awareness of the very existence of these conflicts in far away places and among unknown groups, at least until the conflict becomes the focus of attention by the world media.

Mehraby (2002b) refers to one of the group sessions in which the participants were asked to choose a colored scarf from a pile, as a part of an expressive therapeutic exercise to facilitate the sharing of feelings. They had to choose one scarf of the color they felt reflected or was congruent with or signified their feelings. One of the children, a 13-year-old Hazara boy, picked a red scarf and said "I have chosen this scarf because it is red and red represents blood and I have not seen any thing else but blood during the 13 years of my life" (p. 35).

Mass conflict, whether it is war, civil war, or state terrorism, has a widespread impact on society. Its impact, however, is not necessarily uniform, particularly in the case of civil war and state terrorism. Some groups are severely affected and experience a society vastly different from that they knew before the beginning or exacerbation of the conflict. Others are only marginally affected by the changes. This results in substantial differences in various aspects of the shared norms, values, and beliefs that make up culture. It is not uncommon, therefore, for different "waves" of refugees (or refugees and migrants) from a similar background to differ substantially in their worldview.

We have also encountered significant similarities in worldview and adaptational patterns among refugees from a variety of nationalities and cultural and language backgrounds. Arguably, the stressors and pressures of life in a situation characterized by widespread conflict and/or systematic repression are so important in shaping or modifying behavior patterns, values, and belief systems that they seem to define a subculture of oppression and conflict with almost universal characteristics. This concept might be useful in understanding some of the difficulties encountered by refugees resettling in "civil societies," or indeed, by populations in postconflict situations as central government and the institutions of civil society are reintroduced as part of the reconstruction process.

The Context of the Refugee Experience

One of the issues that makes the experience of refugees so difficult is that their plight does not stop when they are able to flee from their country. For many, this is only the beginning of a long, arduous, and often extremely traumatic process. In the same way that some refugees were born and have matured in a context of war and conflict, some refugees live significant portions of their lives and developmental processes in precarious situations in refugee camps, with uncertain prospects and limited access to essential commodities. The subculture that develops in such permanently transient environments is an important factor in shaping identity and influencing worldviews.

The following excerpt from a news report written 10 years after the first Gulf War about conditions in the Rafha Refugee Camp in Saudi Arabia depicts aspects of this experience.

> While in Saudi Arabia and since, I have heard numerous accounts of human rights violations committed by Saudi soldiers in the camp, including the arbitrary detention, rape, severe beatings and forced repatriation of refugees. While living conditions in Rafha are difficult for everyone, they are particularly bad for women and children. Saudi authorities allow Iraqi refugee women to move about the camp only when fully veiled and in the presence of a male escort. This has a particularly isolating effect on most Iraqi women in the camp, whose modes of dress and social interaction tended to be far more liberal in Iraq. Also deeply troubling is the fact that one-fourth of the camp population are children under the age of 9 who have known nothing but life in the camp. A full 40 percent of the camp population are refugee children under the age of 18. For these children, Rafha is a dead end. (Edminster, 2001)

Similar processes can and do occur in countries of asylum, particularly while asylum seekers are at their most vulnerable waiting for determination of status processes and with limited access to services, and especially in the context of long periods in immigration detention centers. It is at this stage that hostility, discrimination, and prejudice from elements within the host community can cómplicate the always difficult and delicate process of learning to understand and relate to the culture of the new society and exacerbate any existing trauma-related problems.

The Context of Recovery

Understanding the context of recovery is crucial to understanding the person's struggle in the new society and where he or she find him- or herself in the continuum of the cultural transition process that is an inevitable part of resettlement.

In the same way that trauma does not happen in a vacuum, neither does healing. The characteristics of the environment can play extremely important roles in either facilitating or hampering recovery. Ethnocultural issues are crucial at this point. It is at this stage that individuals and families are confronted with a vast array of tasks and demands that are crucial for successful resettlement. One of the most subtle and yet more overwhelming of these demands is learning to understand the new environment, and in particular the language and culture of its people.

The qualities of the environment and its response to the new arrivals influence the course of cultural transition or acculturation that happens inevitably as refugees struggle to understand the new society better. It is not only new norms and social and cultural mores that refugees need to come to terms with, but they must also learn to understand and find their way in a society where they are no longer the target of persecution, and where, as part of civil society, they also have new rights and obligations. At this stage some of the adaptations to life in a war or conflict situation can become maladaptive and could develop into substantial barriers to regaining control of their environment and overcoming the psychological and psychosocial sequelae of trauma. Both government policies and media driven public opinion, as well as cultural proximity, play an important role at this stage and remain a powerful influence on the recovery process of refugees. For example, at the end of 2001, at the height of the much publicized controversial rescue of a group of asylum seekers by the Norwegian freighter *Tampa* from just outside Australia's territorial waters, the media-driven public debate about asylum seekers in Australia reached previously unheard-of levels of passion, resulting in changed public perceptions. Counselors in torture and trauma services reported higher incidence of clients exhibiting symptoms of distress and fears of discrimination and even deportation coinciding with these much publicized events.

Although even permanent residents who arrived as refugees can be affected by these dynamics, asylum seekers and refugees who have been granted temporary protection are particularly vulnerable to the ups and downs of public opinion on refugee issues. Furthermore, asylum seekers and refugees on temporary protection usually experience a much harsher recovery environment, not only in terms of their lack of permanency and stability, and therefore security, but also in terms of limited access to services and restricted rights. The ultimate expression of this, of course, is the restriction of their liberty, as in the case of asylum seekers subjected to mandatory detention in immigration detention facilities (such as those arriving in an "unauthorized fashion" to Australia).

As Silove (2002) points out

> Asylum seekers are trapped in a continuum of threat, with conditions fostering a convergence and compounding of insecurities from the past, present and future. Memories of past dangers and humiliations intermingle with current feelings of uncertainty; this, in turn, magnifies fears of future persecution should detainees be repatriated. Recollections of past imprisonment merge with recurrent feelings of outrage at being confined behind razor wire in the country in which the asylum seeker has sought freedom. Loss of control over one's personal life, an inescapable reality when living under repressive governments, is compounded by the regime of control in the detention centre. The future is perceived as being entirely in the hands of an impersonal bureaucracy, intensifying feelings of helplessness. (p. 294)

The situation of asylum seekers, refugees in temporary protection, and even more so, that of detained asylum seekers confronts agencies and clinicians with complex ethical and ethnocultural dilemmas, since for many or our clients in this sort of situation, the clinician and the agency can be seen as extensions of the host culture and society that can be perceived as hostile and unhelpful.

UNDERSTANDING THE MULTIPLE LEVELS, MEANINGS, AND CONSEQUENCES OF COMPLEX TRAUMA

About Culture, Social Systems and Sociopolitical Background

As the treatment of torture and refugee trauma developed as a field worldwide, the utilization of approaches incorporating interventions at various levels of the social systems have become more widespread. Thus, although individual treatment is still the treatment of choice in many instances, family and group interventions, interventions targeting community structures, and interventions focused on improving the interface between different refugee communities and the mainstream society have become a lot more common.

Trauma and the dislocation that characterizes the refugee experience affects people as individuals, as families, and in terms of their immediate reference groups, as well as in their relation with their immediate community and the community at large. A range of interventions have been developed that address issues and needs at these various levels and contribute to enhance their role as social support and cultural reference structures. Figure 4.1 (Aroche & Coello, 1994) offers examples of

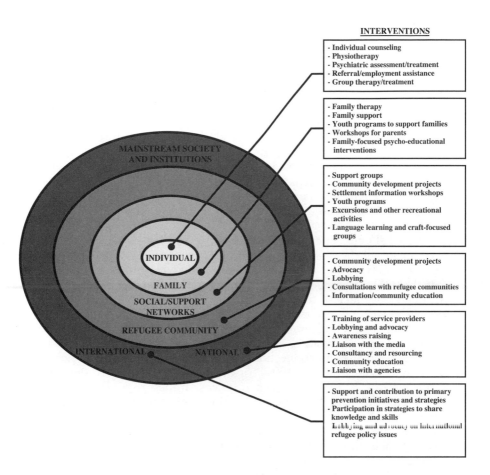

INTERVENTIONS

- Individual counseling
- Physiotherapy
- Psychiatric assessment/treatment
- Referral/employment assistance
- Group therapy/treatment

- Family therapy
- Family support
- Youth programs to support families
- Workshops for parents
- Family-focused psycho-educational
  interventions

- Support groups
- Community development projects
- Settlement information workshops
- Youth programs
- Excursions and other recreational
  activities
- Language learning and craft-focused
  groups

- Community development projects
- Advocacy
- Lobbying
- Consultations with refugee communities
- Information/community education

- Training of service providers
- Lobbying and advocacy
- Awareness raising
- Liaison with the media
- Consultancy and resourcing
- Community education
- Liaison with agencies

- Support and contribution to primary
  prevention initiatives and strategies
- Participation in strategies to share
  knowledge and skills
- Lobbying and advocacy on international
  refugee policy issues

Fig. 4.1 Appropriate Interventions With Refugee Populations

appropriate interventions with refugee populations focusing on various levels of the system.

From an ethnocultural point of view it is important to keep in mind that a complex array of tensions play themselves within and between these levels in the system. Within the family, for example, different individuals are likely to become acculturated at different rates, depending on age, gender, and circumstance. The resulting tensions and anxieties can play an important role in the expression of symptoms associated with traumatic events experienced prior to resettlement. Understanding the problems of refugees involves an appreciation of the interface between these factors.

About Trauma, Ethnocultural Issues, and PTSD

Not all refugees who have survived harrowing experiences involving trauma in the context of organized violence, or even torture, suffer psychological problems associated with these experiences. Many do, however. Steel (2001), in a recent literature review about the validity of posttraumatic stress disorder (PTSD) with refugee populations, observed that the prevalence of PTSD among refugee populations documented by 14 independent studies ranged from 3.5 to 100%. In terms of the cultural relevance of PTSD, Steel identified two diverging views in the literature; one that argued that psychological traumatization and its aftermath will be the most important factor impeding reconstruction efforts in postconflict situations, and an opposing view that identifies trauma and PTSD as concepts imposed by Western traumatologists on postwar indigenous populations in what amounts to a new form of cultural imperialism.

The PTSD concept has also been criticized for its failure to fully account for all the changes and comorbid presentations that are common among torture survivors and otherwise traumatized refugees (Steel, 2001). Other views, such as that exposed by Eisenbruch (1991), maintain that much of the symptomatology and comorbid presentations associated with refugee trauma is better understood in the context of a process he coined "cultural bereavement," which relates to the loss of home, material possessions, social networks, and the sense of social and spiritual belonging and connection to a land, its symbols, and its people.

Friedman and Jaranson (1994), on an earlier exploration of the applicability of the PTSD concept to refugees, argued that although "the PTSD model is useful in conceptualizing the traumatic experience of refugees ... it must be broadened to incorporate ethnocultural differences in the expression of traumatic stress" (p. 216). They further assert that although "the pattern of co-morbid diagnoses may change from one setting to another, ... such variations do not invalidate the PTSD as a conceptual approach," and conclude that despite various valid criticisms of the PTSD concept, it still "offers a useful conceptual and therapeutic approach to the psychological impact of trauma on refugees from all ethnocultural backgrounds" (p. 221).

Our views concur with the above statement by Friedman and Jaranson (1994) about the ongoing usefulness of the PTSD concept. It can also be argued that the relevance of arguments based on the resonance of the PTSD concept to indigenous populations in postconflict situations is questionable in the case of populations like refugees and asylum seekers who are outside their country of origin and thus engaged, however reluctantly, in a process of cultural transition.

A full discussion of the applicability of PTSD across cultures is, however, outside the scope of this chapter. Despite the ongoing controversy in academic fora, the minutiae of the arguments about the cross-cultural validity of PTSD are of questionable relevance to the practicing clinician (and even more so to helpers engaged in psychosocial interventions). Few refugee clients, indeed, few clients at all, relate readily to PTSD or any other diagnostic criteria. Yet these constructs still provide useful tools for clinicians to understand and exchange knowledge and ideas that can lead to better outcomes for clients seeking help for their perceived problems (Jaranson, 1998; Steel, 2001). The challenge for the clinician remains to be able to utilize constructs such as PTSD to inform his or her clinical practice, while retaining a flexible approach to the interpretation of signs of distress possibly connected with the traumatic events undergone in the context of the refugee experience.

From this perspective, one of the inherent limitations of conceptualizing the problems of refugees and asylum seekers in terms of PTSD or even "cultural bereavement" is that both constructs tend to explain the current problems of refugees in terms of events that took place in the past, as courses set in motion, which can be managed or treated, but not prevented.

Our belief is that most of the problems commonly exhibited by refugee and asylum seekers are the result of a dynamic interaction between trauma-related or posttraumatic issues, the stresses and demands of the exile, the migration and resettlement process, and other stressors that affect refugees much the same way they affect the rest of the population (Aroche & Coello, 1994). These factors, as diagrammed in Figure 4.2, are likely to interact in powerful and complex ways.

> It is precisely the complex interface between these factors on the canvas formed by the psychological, cultural, educational and religious attributes or baggage of the individual, family or community that can be best said to define the predicaments that refugees confront in exile. (Aroche & Coello, 1994, p. 1)

The advantage of this conceptualization is that it introduces scope for the prevention of many of the perceived problems experienced by refugees and asylum seekers, as it provides a framework to devise interventions to defuse the complexity and power of the interface between these factors. In this context, concepts such as PTSD and "cultural bereavement" become most useful to understand the contributing factors in complex presentations. Ethnocultural issues associated with cultural differences and incompatible worldviews play a crucial role in these complex interactions, and account for much of the sense of loss of control and confusion experienced by refugees and asylum seekers in first world countries. The therapeutic relationship, as well as targeted psychosocial interventions, provides an excellent forum to explore ethnocultural issues and thus contributes to improve aspects of this interface.

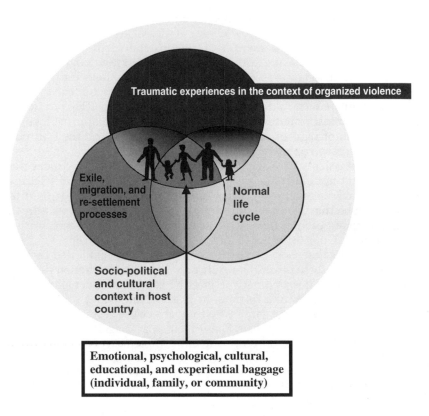

Fig. 4.2 Interaction of Issues Affecting Refugee and Asylum Seekers

OVERCOMING BARRIERS TO SERVICE DELIVERY

Creating the context for effective therapeutic or psychosocial interventions with refugees inevitably involves overcoming language and cultural differences that can easily become barriers. More accurately, working with refugees involves building multiple bridges to overcome these differences and to enable the therapeutic work to take place. This still holds true to a lesser extent even when the therapist comes from the same ethnocultural background and speaks the same language.

A variety of approaches have been utilized to facilitate work across language (and cultural) differences. Effective therapeutic work can and has been achieved, with the assistance of qualified interpreters, by bilingual paraprofessionals supported by mainstream professionals, by bilingual professionals, and by relying on the clients own knowledge of the language spoken by the therapist. In some cases, bilingual professionals or paraprofessionals can also provide the added benefit of having an in-depth understanding of the culture associated with the particular language.

Regardless of which approach is applied, there is always a cultural chasm that must be bridged, and potential power issues that must be kept in mind. The following observations apply in most cases:

- **Nationality:** Country of origin and nationality are not always synonymous, particularly in the case of refugees, who might belong to a particular minority, or stateless nation (e.g., Kurdish). Because of the pressures involved in conforming to a legal and bureaucratic system that emphasizes country of birth as the main identifier, refugee clients might not always spontaneously identify themselves in terms of their first preference. It is important to address this issue proactively and ensure that issues of nationality and preferred national identity are discussed early in the course of the intervention.
- **Language:** Country of birth and proficiency in the mainstream language of that nation do not always go together. Since preferred language is usually intimately associated with the client's ethnocultural identity, some clients might prefer to use a minority language in which they feel more comfortable. This can be either because they are more proficient in it or because of the political connotations associated with that language (e.g., it is seen as the language of the struggle for his or her ethnocultural group). Alternatively, clients might not prefer to use a language in which they are fluent if this is seen as the language of the oppressor. Similar considerations apply with clients who might be sufficiently fluent in the language of the host nation to communicate with the helper without language assistance. Therefore, it is important to clarify the preferred language and its ethnocultural and sociopolitical implications early in the intervention, and whether or not they ultimately influence the choice of language to be used. For example, engaging an interpreter in a little-known and little-used language might not be a possible or cost-effective option with a client who fluently speaks the language of the host country or a more easily available language. Addressing these issues to clarify and discuss the client's motivation and the inherent limitations of the system can fulfill a very important function and assist the client to develop more sophisticated constructs to deal with dilemmas involving power issues and ethnocultural issues affecting their communication needs.
- **Confidentiality and community politics issues:** Confidentiality and trust issues are also important factors in deciding the best method to overcome language barriers. Clients from some small communities, particularly from societies fragmented by conflict, might prefer to do without an interpreter, or opt for an interpreter from another community in a language in which they are not as proficient. This can be motivated by a desire to avoid the risk of other community members learning about their histories. Alternatively, they might wish to avoid

a potential encounter with a person from the group associated with their repression in the country of origin who they perceive as capable of compromising their safety or that of family members still in the country of origin. This decision can also be deeply connected with ethnocultural issues and the client's cultural transition process (which can happen at a different rate than the acquisition of the language of the host country). Thus, a client who is ready to deal with issues that might be heavily stigmatized in their original culture might prefer to do this in a context that creates some "distance" from that culture as represented by their local community.

- **Gender:** A history of politically sanctioned gender violence can also be an issue in the choice of therapist and interpreter. Similarly, it might not feel appropriate for some clients to discuss certain issues with a person of the opposite sex, or even to meet in private. Again, such issues can be perceived as more important than language or cultural proximity in this choice.

- **Mixed marriages:** Mixed marriages, particularly between spouses from opposing sides in an ethnic or religious conflict, often pose interesting dilemmas in terms of the choice of therapist or interpreter. Provided a degree of safety can be guaranteed by the counselor, open discussion and clarification of these issues at the beginning of the intervention is useful and can be helpful in addressing identity and trust issues that can become significant later on.

- **Religion:** Religion can range from being central to the choice of helper or interpreter to being irrelevant, depending on the nature of the conflict associated with the client's refugee experience. Although it is not necessary to share the client's religious beliefs to provide an effective clinical intervention, it is certainly desirable to possess a basic understanding of the precepts and philosophical tenets of the religion in question. For many people, religion plays a central role in how they interpret their lives and experiences, and it influences the nature of the metaphors and construction of meaning that take place in therapy.

- **Length of stay in the country and degree of acculturation:** The length of stay in the host country and the degree of acculturation can often be issues for newly arrived refugees from certain countries, either because the time of arrival can correlate with particular push factors in the country of origin associated with political positions or persuasions (e.g., Chileans who left Chile before and after the fall of the Allende government) or simply because of ethnocultural differences associated with the passage of time and accentuated by splits in community politics associated with local issues.

- **Role of the ongoing conflict:** Because of their personal commitment to a particular cause, and because of concerns about the safety of friends and family and kinship ties back to their country of origin, refugees are particularly likely to be affected by changes in circumstances and developments in the conflict in their country of origin. These issues have the potential to not only trigger or exacerbate posttraumatic symptoms and grief reactions, but also to introduce changes in how refugees and asylum seekers see themselves in their new society and in their beliefs about how the new society regards them. This is particularly relevant in situations where the host country is involved or is perceived to influence events in their country of origin or in the region.

- **Public opinion in the host country:** Media coverage about the ongoing conflict or local incidents involving particular communities can bring about rapid real or perceived changes in public opinion that can in turn affect refugee client's perception of the safety and supportiveness of their environment. Incidents of racism or discrimination, in particular, are not only retraumatizing in their own right, and therefore potentially associated with a relapse or exacerbation in posttraumatic symptoms, but can also affect the quality of the relationship with the helper and the need to revisit safety and trust issues and associated ethnocultural concerns.

- **Local refugee community politics:** The tenor of local refugee community politics can range from the sublimely benign to the absolutely vicious. At their best, refugee communities can offer their members an unparallel means of support and of cultural reference in an alien environment. At times, however, they can also be a source of pressure and unrealistic expectations to conform to cultural values and/or hold sociopolitical or worldview positions that can no longer be consonant with those held by newly arrived refugees and asylum seekers. It is also important to note that both interpreters and bilingual paraprofessionals and professionals can be subjected to similar pressures.

- **Cultural competence and sensitivity:** Language and culture might not necessarily be synonymous with cultural competence, as described by "the set of academic and interpersonal skills that allow individuals to increase their understanding and appreciation of cultural differences and similarities within, among and between groups" (Orlandi, 1995). Unfortunately, there is often a temptation, both among bilingual and nonbilingual professionals and paraprofessionals, to assume an inexorable link between language and cultural competence and sensitivity. Hence, it is important to explore this assumption and apply the same criteria to both groups.

THE PRAGMATICS OF SERVICE DELIVERY

Bilingual Professionals

Bilingual professionals with relevant training, qualifications, and experience are undoubtedly the most direct and effective way to bridge language barriers. Assuming that this automatically bridges cultural differences, however, is not warranted, and bilingual professionals need to pay attention to the same considerations as mainstream professionals.

Even when the therapist and the client share a similar nationality and cultural background, subtle ethnocultural issues still arise in the context of countries of asylum that need to be recognized and addressed in the therapeutic relationship. These might relate to local and regional differences, ethnocultural differences (where the client and the therapist belong to different ethnic or religious groups), differences in political affiliation, and socioeconomic class, and just as important, differences in terms of the amount of time residing in the host country. Depending on the nature of these differences and the characteristic of the conflict, the therapist can be construed as being associated with a particular persuasion in the conflict, and these issues might need to be proactively addressed early in the therapeutic relationship.

There is also the potential risk, all too common, even among experienced therapists, to assume that one's own firsthand appreciation of the issues involved in a conflict reflects that of the client.

Bilingual Paraprofessionals

Similar issues apply to paraprofessionals as they do to professionals. There are, however, additional issues that are particularly important to consider in terms of their ethnocultural implications.

Paraprofessionals usually work in cotherapy with suitably qualified counselors or therapists, or closely supervised by them (Becker et al. 1990; Bowles, 2001; Mehraby, 2002a). In most of these situations there is an understanding, formal or tacit, about the mutual role each plays in this partnership. Usually, this means that the paraprofessional contributes his or her language and cultural knowledge and skills, as well as his or her relevant life experience to the therapeutic dyad, while the professional contributes his or her clinical training, skills, and experience. There is always, however, a power differential within this relationship, reinforced by differences in work conditions, status, and pay.

Although this complementary arrangement can work extremely well and very effectively when there is good rapport, cooperation, and understanding between both members of the dyad, it can be fraught with problems when this is not so. Any such relationship has the potential to mirror in the context of the therapy the power dynamics between the host community and the refugee community. Thus, a harmonious and respectful relationship can help model positive community relationships and assist clients to work through some of the inherent power issues involved in learning to navigate their way in a new society. At the same time, any unresolved power issues and tensions within the therapeutic dyad are likely to be picked up by the client and can become symbolic of community relationships at large, thus reinforcing disempowering constructions about their role in the new society.

In order to ensure that this approach can work effectively it is essential for the therapeutic dyad to pay close attention to these issues in an environment that promotes open discussion. Clinical supervision that addresses power dynamics and challenges assumptions about prescribed roles and ethnocultural issues can also contribute significantly to the system working well. It is also important to ensure that the organization is able to provide some protection from possible unreasonable demands from their ethnic community related to their professional role, and thus shield them from burnout. One way to ensure that the system does not stagnate and the organizational culture continues to move in a direction that encourages empowering community and race relations is to openly acknowledge this model as a second best, and to adopt a commitment as an organization to work to encourage paraprofessionals to develop their skills so as to become professional therapists in their own right.

Interpreters

The situation with professional interpreters is, from an ethnocultural perspective, somewhat different, but not less complex. Unlike health care paraprofessionals, interpreters have a more prescribed role within the therapeutic dyad. They usually have no aspirations or interest in becoming therapists and are usually part of a quite separate professional network and association, with their own professional codes and standards. It is still possible, however, for power issues along ethnocultural lines to play themselves in the therapist-interpreter-client triangle. It is essential, therefore, for the therapist to be alert to this possibility and prepared to intervene early to defuse dynamics that can be disempowering of the client or counterproductive in terms of the intended outcomes for the intervention.

Interpreters often play a tacit role as "cultural translators" or "cultural aides." This can be a very useful role that can contribute significantly to the cultural appropriateness and effectiveness of the intervention, but which can also place the therapist and the therapy in a compromised position for many of the reasons raised earlier in this section.

MAKING INTERVENTIONS WORK ACROSS THE ETHNOCULTURAL DIVIDE

What treatment is more likely to be successful in terms of achieving the clinical outcomes identified, and improving the quality of life of the client or group of clients? What makes a treatment acceptable or culturally appropriate to a particular group of refugee clients? Indeed, is any of what Western psychology has to offer relevant and acceptable, not to mention appropriate, when working with clients from such different cultures and worldviews?

These are questions that every clinician working with refugees has asked him- or herself at least once, and hopefully many times. There are no definitive answers, yet the questions remain valid for every client we see.

As the torture and trauma field matured, no treatment of choice for the problems exhibited by traumatized refugees and asylum seekers has emerged, either in terms of effectiveness as clinical tools or cultural appropriateness. Numerous clinicians and researchers have reported on the implementation of various approaches with seemingly positive results and no stated problems in terms of their acceptance by refugee groups or their cultural appropriateness (Jaranson, 1998; van der Veer, 1993). The lack of a treatment of choice is hardly surprising given the diversity of refugees and asylum seekers as a group and the variety of clinical presentations encountered. This is not to say, however, that any treatment is likely to work or to be accepted by this population. Rather, it is suggested that *how* the treatment is provided might be more important than the kind of treatment selected, provided it fits the perceived problem and worldview of the client.

The rest of this section provides some practical considerations for maximizing the effectiveness and appropriateness of interventions with traumatized refugees.

Clinical Interventions

Treatment Environment

The environment where treatment takes place is important, both because it is likely to provide the very first impression about the therapist and the agency he or she represents, and because it provides important clues about the quality of the personal or agency commitment to the client.

An environment that appears flexible and fairly informal, that places the comfort and needs of the client in a high priority, and that portrays, through its décor and ambience, a readiness to be inspired by other cultural influences provides a good start.

As van der Veer (1993) suggests, every contact with the agency is important, from the welcome at the waiting room to the phone contact with the receptionist, as it conveys the positive regard and respect that is an essential aspect of cultural sensitivity. Cold, bureaucratic-looking environments where security features are prominent (as is the case in many hospital and mental health settings) tend to provide a nonverbal message that introduces distance between the client and the agency (and the therapist), which can be difficult to overcome in the therapy session.

Pretreatment Phase

It is important to ensure that the referral procedures are structured to elicit information that makes it possible to make informed decisions about the best choice of therapist and interpreter (where relevant). Adequate information is also important in terms of dealing preemptively with as many of the possible cultural barriers discussed earlier in this chapter.

Accurate information about the background of the client also makes it possible to conduct some preliminary research about cultural and sociopolitical issues that can be important in understanding the context of the client's refugee experience and current situation.

First Contact

The first contact with the agency can be a puzzling and unsettling experience for the client, who might be unsure of the reason for his or her referral and the possible benefits of contact with a counselor. This is particularly the case with clients from cultures where Western style "talking" therapies are not common. There can also be an element of fear of the unknown. It is quite possible that the session with the therapist might be the closest encounter the client has had with a "representative" from the culture of the host country.

It is important, therefore, that the first session enables the client to regain some measure of control over the situation and provides the space to clarify the purpose of the intervention, the motivation of the counselor and the agency, the expectations of both client and therapist, and the closest equivalent to this process in the client's cultural frame of reference. It can be important at this stage to be somewhat pro-active in offering information about the agency, and creating the space for the client to ask questions or venture information about him- or herself and his or her cultural background.

This is also the time to check the validity of the assumptions made at the time of referral about language and cultural issues impacting the choice of therapist, interpreter, and any other relevant variables. This can include reflecting on our own suitability as the therapist for this client. A modicum of information about the cultural and sociopolitical background of the client places the therapist in a better position to ask questions that are relevant and significant to the construction of shared meaning about the intervention.

Assessment and Intervention

Consonant with the above-expressed views about the multifactorial character of the problems experienced by refugees and asylum seekers in resettlement countries, we believe that a clinical assessment should attempt to explore the relative impact of these factors on the presenting problem. In particular, it should attempt to ascertain the role of traumatic events that occurred in the context of the refugee experience from that of ongoing stressors associated with the resettlement process and the normal life cycle that might be further complicating the picture, yet be more amenable to practical interventions.

A full discussion of clinical aspects of the assessment phase is outside the scope of this chapter (see Chapter 5 for further discussion of this). From an ethnocultural perspective, however, it is important to emphasize the need to be attentive to possible culture-bound idiomatic and nonverbal expressions relevant to the presenting problem. It is also vital to ensure that the approach, protocol, or procedure in use allows the therapist to explore ethnocultural issues that can impact the presenting problem or significant areas of the client's life and identity. The assessment process should also allow space to explore the impact of critical settlement, cultural transition, and ethnocultural issues at various levels of the system, as outlined in Table 4.1.

If therapy is a shared process of constructing meaning in a way that enables clients to tap inner resources to gain control over their symptoms and ultimately their lives, it necessarily relies on an exchange of communications imbued with particular meaning relevant to the cultural frame of reference of the parties involved. It is to be expected that at certain junctures in this process ethnocultural issues and dilemmas will come to the forefront of the communication in the form of metaphors, symbols, and behaviors that will alternatively challenge the therapist and the client. At times these can relate to culture in the orthodox sense. At other times, these can rely heavily on sociopolitical codes. Throughout the intervention it is essential to continue to pay attention to these issues and remain open and willing to learn from clients in order to find common ground that enables communication to move forward.

It is equally important to ensure that ethnocultural and sociopolitical issues are addressed in clinical supervision, particularly given that inevitably, ethnocultural issues are likely to be expressed in transference and countertransference dynamics.

Clinical Supervision

Clinical supervision is essential to support counselors working with refugees in a clinical setting, both because of the impact of trauma and also to assist counselors to navigate through the many ethnocultural issues that surface in the therapeutic relationship. There is also a need for a similar process to support workers engaged in psychosocial interventions with refugee groups and communities.

In addition to other issues normally addressed in supervision, it is important that the clinical supervisor explores countertransference dynamics in relation to ethnocultural issues, discussing the counselor's constructions about the impact of the client's worldview and culture on

TABLE 4.1 Ethnoculttural Issues in Assessment

Level	Issues to Explore
Individual	Explore cultural/religious/ethnic identity issues.
Immediate family	Ascertain level of acculturation and language proficiency (host country and country of origin) of individuals within the family. Assess extent to which the cultural transition process is affecting family dynamics. Assess mixed marriages issues. Assess issues with family remaining overseas.
Refugee community	Assess cultural distance issues between individual/family and community in host country. Assess to what extent community from country of origin constitutes a support structure and availability and appropriateness of the same.
Mainstream society	Assess extent to which current government policies and media coverage of conflict facilitates or hinders resettlement and positive attitude toward client group. Assess client's perceptions of host society and his or her perception of how he or she is seen. Assess whether racism and discrimination are present and the extent of impact on client and family.
International	Assess the extent to which the course of the conflict is actively affecting client's emotional state. Find out how immediate family, friends, and ethnocultural reference group are being affected by the course of the conflict in the country of origin.

the therapeutic relationship and assisting the counselor in monitoring the client's perceptions of the intervention and its value.

Thus, clinical supervision can assist counselors to maintain a balanced position in their dealing with ethnocultural issues encountered in therapy, therefore avoiding the common pitfalls of either magnifying or minimizing the importance of culture.

Clinical supervision can also be critical as a means of supporting and grounding staff at times such as those mentioned elsewhere in this chapter, when sociopolitical factors, such as worsening racial relations or unfavorable media attention focused on refugees, exacerbate the client's distress associated with ethnocultural issues, and their tendency to make negative projections in this respect toward the counselor.

Psychosocial Interventions and Adjuncts to Therapy

As Silove and Ekblad (2002) suggest,

> Providing effective and humane resettlement services, clarifying refugee claims in a timely manner, encouraging family reunion, countering tendencies towards racism and xenophobia in the wider society, offering opportunities for work and education, and providing targeted mental health interventions for the most psychologically needy, together will ensure that most refugees regain their capacity for self-sufficiency and productivity, an outcome that will benefit refugees themselves as well as the receiving societies. (p. 402)

Because of the complexity of the resettlement and cultural transition processes and their impact on just about every aspect of the lives of refugees and asylum seekers, it is sometimes appropriate to develop interventions specifically designed to provide a space for refugee clients to explore these issues in a supportive environment that propitiates the development of better conceptual tools to understand and negotiate the new culture and society. Examples of such interventions developed at STARTTS include the Families in Cultural Transitions Program (FICT), STARTTS' youth program, and various support groups (see Figures 4.3, 4.4, and 4.5 for a description of these programs).

Ethnocultural and sociopolitical considerations are just as important to the process of planning and implementing community-based psychosocial interventions. In fact, there is an added layer of complexity associated with understanding the group dynamics and power issues that play themselves within refugee communities and the interactions between refugee community politics and mainstream society.

The Role of the Agency

The agency plays a central role in providing counselors and other staff with an environment that is conducive to positive race relations and that fosters and supports a genuine interest in understanding and working with new and emerging refugee communities. It can also provide the structure to hold and support its staff (particularly those from refugee communities themselves), who might be more susceptible to the pressures and demands from their communities and to assist them in preserving the integrity of professional and personal boundaries, which are essential to prevent vicarious traumatization and burnout.

In order to achieve this, a genuine commitment from senior management to meet refugee clients and refugee communities "on their own turf" is necessary. This must be proactively expressed in terms of positive staff relations and an organizational culture that celebrates diversity and is genuinely committed to fair employment practices and equal opportunity. It is only by ensuring that race relations within the agency model the best practice and embody the stated values of the agency that

Families in Cultural Transitions (FICT) Program

The program was originally conceived through the process of running a series of experimental workshops conducted with newly arrived refugees at a migrant hostel. The content of these interactive workshops developed organically around the main issues affecting the participants' resettlement, and in particular, their impact on family dynamics. The workshops focused primarily on assisting refugees to develop a more functional conceptual framework about life in Australia and the effect of the exile, migration, and resettlement process on them and their families. Thus they would be better equipped to face the challenges and demands of resettlement and the interaction with the effects of previous traumatic experiences.

Building on the ideas and material developed on this early experimental phase, the FICT covers a variety of topics that tend to pose considerable challenges to refugees settling in Australia. The approach adopted is largely psychoeducational, with a heavy emphasis on making the workshops fun and highly interactive. To this effect, two board games and a number of group exercises and structured activities have been specifically designed to address issues in a sensitive and nonconfrontational manner that maximizes the participants ability to explore and adjust their assumptive world.

The FICT kit has been designed to enable nonclinicians with group work skills to conduct FICT programs easily and effectively. The kit consists of two board games and nine chapters that discuss the rationale for addressing each topic and provide the trainer with methods, ideas, and group activities to explore these topics with the participants. The chapters address the following issues: the settlement process itself, support systems, money issues, trauma and healing, issues for families, issues for children, gender issues, youth issues, and enjoying the new environment. The program has been designed to be conducted over ten 3.5-hour sessions, although alternative ways of covering the material have been considered in its development and implemented. Shortened versions of this program have also been presented.

The program has now been successfully implemented with a large variety of refugee groups from diverse cultural and linguistic backgrounds in different settings, largely through the development of a panel of bicultural and bilingual facilitators specifically trained for this purpose, and through partnerships with institutions such the NSW Department of School Education, the NSW Department of Technical and Further Education, and institutions teaching English as a second language.

The program has been designed to be easily adaptable across cultures, as it relies on experiential group processes rather than prescriptions. Its successful use across cultures as varied as Spanish speaking, Arabic and Persian speakers, African communities, Indochinese (Vietnam, Cambodia, Laos), Serbian and Bosnian and East Timorese attest to its potential as a cross-cultural intervention.

The preliminary results of an evaluation study of the effectiveness of this program indicates that the four main advantages of using the FICT program as a method of intervention with people from varied refugee backgrounds are:

• Reduction in feelings of isolation and alienation
• Normalization of responses
• Increased motivation and perception of self-efficacy
• Creation of a supportive network

The very positive feedback from communities and participants has also been most encouraging (Aroche, Coello, & Hartgerink, 2000, pp. 7–8).

Fig. 4.3 Example of Intervention Program Developed at STARTTS—FICT

Group Programs

Social isolation and the absence of effective support networks are common complaints of refugees settling in Australia. This often results from the combination of difficulties in trusting other people and organizations and the lack of opportunity to make contact with people that share common interests, common language, and a compatible worldview.

The presence of effective support networks has been found to be a protective factor in recovery from trauma. There is no reason to doubt that this also applies to refugees settling in a new country, and that effective social and support networks can play an important role in preventing some of the problems we often see in the postresettlement period.

STARTTS groups program employs various strategies to bring people from compatible and refugee situations together in a supportive environment. In order to be successful, the groups must come together around a common interest that is both attractive and not too confronting. Finding such a common interest is often one of the major challenges faced in establishing support groups.

The support groups held at STARTTS may start in many different ways, ranging from those starting around information sessions and group outings, or skill-related classes (sewing, computer skills, etc.), to such activities as soccer, informal coffee bar groups, or the development of a community garden.

The crucial aspect of this strategy is the development of a situation where people feel comfortable to come together in an environment that is perceived as safe, caring, and reassuring. To begin with, these groups tend to rely on the staff facilitator to a considerable extent and are seldom effective without the committed presence of a staff member.

Over time, however, many of these groups develop strong informal and even formal structures and become less reliant on staff support. This progression can be seen as both a measure of success for the group as a strategy, but is also evidence of increased confidence among its members.

Another significant aspect of support groups in relation to prevention and early intervention work is their psychoeducation and symptom normalization focus. Some of this input is provided by the group facilitator, but often the awareness that other group members are experiencing similar psychosocial difficulties is reassuring and helpful.

Our clinical observations also support the value of people attending activities as part of our support group program as an adjunct to clinical interventions.

From a prevention perspective, however, the fact that people continue to attend such groups and often develop friendships in that context, is a significant achievement.

Fig. 4.4 Examples of Intervention Programs Developed at STARTTS—Group (Aroche, Coello, & Hartgerink, 2000, pp. 9–10)

a genuine sense of respect for the culture and issues of clients can be conveyed. Furthermore, successfully meeting the challenges involved in managing an agency employing culturally diverse staff in a consultative and inclusive manner provides the best training ground for working effectively as an agency with refugee communities.

It is also important for the organization to play an appropriate and identifiable role in the life of the community, by being represented at community events, by participating in relevant networking activities,

Youth Programs

Many children and young people in our client group present with specific problems in connection with their exposure to traumatic situations. In addition to these particular problems, they often face difficult family situations associated with their parents' posttraumatic symptomatology and settlement-related problems. They often experience these difficulties in isolation.

The youth program aims to assist young refugees aged between 10 and 18 years deal with the impact of torture and trauma experiences and resettlement issues. It also aims to assist young refugees to conceptualize and deal with cultural and intergenerational issues that arise between them and their parents. The program provides an environment where young people can explore new interests, try out new behaviors, and develop friendships with other young people from similar backgrounds.

This aim has been met through a range of strategies, including residential and camp programs for groups of young people aged between 10 to 13 and 14 to 18 years, which provide participants with activities designed to explore their identity, validate and normalize their experiences and feelings, and improve communication skills.

Outdoor settings and activities provide an opportunity to push the boundaries of their fears and perceived limitations, develop teamwork and leadership skills, and increase self-esteem. They also provide a fun environment where children can explore new ways of relating and try different activities and interests that would not normally be accessible to them.

STARTTS has also supported the establishment of youth groups for newly arrived refugee communities as a means of mediating the process of cultural adaptation, and provide additional opportunities for young people to develop friendships and support networks. A variety of innovative programs developed and implemented in partnership with the NSW school system have greatly enhanced the scope and accessibility of focused interventions for young refugees.

As a preventative strategy, the youth program aims to provide young refugees with skills that will help them to face some of the difficulties inherent to the settlement process. They also provide an excellent opportunity to identify early-on individual young people who may be experiencing difficulties, and offer them access to more targeted interventions.

Fig. 4.5 Examples of Intervention Programs Developed at STARTTS—Youth (Aroche, Coello, & Hartgerink, 2000, pp. 11–12)

and by engaging in formal and informal consultation processes with relevant communities. These processes are useful at many levels, in terms of

1. the feedback and ideas received from participants that can result in improved service delivery and a better fit with the needs and aspirations of the community,
2. the improved awareness within the refugee community about the services offered by the agency and its ethical position, which often results in more positive expectations from clients referred into counseling or other interventions; and

3. the outcomes of the process itself, which constructs a space for community members to express their needs, ideas, and grievances about the agency, and to receive feedback about these issues, thus empowering the refugee community in relation to the agency.

Another important role of the agency is to act as a conduit or advocate for issues affecting refugee communities identified in the course of its everyday work and through activities such as community consultations. This role not only fulfills an important function in terms of contributing to mediate changes that have the potential to influence the recovery environment, but also facilitates the role of the therapist in dealing with these issues with the client. Essentially, it makes it possible for the therapist to respond to client issues without compromising therapeutic boundaries, as the advocacy role is passed on to the agency.

SUMMARY

Refugees and asylum seekers present as a complex and diverse group. Working with traumatized refugees requires the clinician not only to face distressing stories and complicated clinical and psychosocial situations, but also a minefield of language, ethnocultural, sociopolitical, and community politics issues. Ethnocultural and related issues are not just the background, but are often at the forefront of perceived client problems. It is not uncommon for counselors, therapists, and helpers in general to feel overwhelmed and ineffective. "Freezing" into inaction for fear of making mistakes in the unfamiliar cultural context or opting to ignore these complexities altogether and rely on the client to bridge the cultural divide are frequent mistakes made by counselors in these situations.

Taking ethnocultural and related issues seriously and factoring them into the planning and implementation phase of any intervention are essential aspects of working with traumatized refugees in an ethical, professional, and effective manner. The implications are many for both individual practitioners and the institutions engaged in this work. They involve assigning time and resources to develop skills to handle these issues more effectively and, in the case of organizations, to also ensure that this commitment is backed by appropriate policies and procedures to ensure consistent standards across the agency.

It is even more essential, however, to ensure that confronting ethnocultural and related issues does not become an end in itself, but rather a means to promote recovery and healing. Addressing ethnocultural issues, therefore, is best done side by side with clients to build cultural bridges that can be expanded from the intervention to other areas of their lives. In the end, we are all human, and the similarities are far greater than the differences. Refugees are in an ongoing process of cultural transition and, therefore, quite inclined to forgive cultural gaffes, and our genuine interest and respect remain the most effective tools in building trust and positive regard across cultural barriers.

REFERENCES

Aroche, J., & Coello, M. (1994, December 5–9). *Toward a systemic approach for the treatment and rehabilitation of torture and trauma survivors in exile: The experience of STARTTS in Australia.* Paper presented at the fourth International Conference of Centres, Institutions and Individuals Concerned with Victims of Organized Violence, Caring for and Empowering Victims of Human Rights Violations, Dap Tageytay City, Philippines.

Aroche, J., Coello, M., & Hartgerink, P. (2000, March 16–19). *Early intervention programs for the prevention of psychosocial disability in traumatised refugees resettling in Australia.* Paper presented at the third World Conference for the International Society for Traumatic Stress Studies (ISTSS), Melbourne, Australia.

Becker, R., Haidary, Z., Kang, V., Marin, L., Nguyen, T., Phraxayavong, V., et al. (1991). The two-practitioner model: Bicultural workers in a service for torture and trauma survivors. In P. Hosking (Ed.), *Hope after horror* (pp. 138–156). Uniya, Melbourne, Vic.

Bowles, R. (2001). Social work with refugee survivors of torture and trauma. In M. Alston & J. McKinnon (Eds.), *Social works fields of practice.* Melbourne, Australia: Oxford University Press.

Edminster, S. (2001, September 10). News NGWRC Web (National Gulf War Resource Center, Inc.). http://www.iraqfoundation.org/news/2001/iseptember/5_saudi.html

Eisenbruch, M. (1991). From post-traumatic stress disorder to cultural bereavement: Diagnosis of Southeast Asian refugees. *Social Science & Medicine, 33,* 673–680.

Farbey, J. (2002). The refugee condition: Legal and therapeutic dimensions. In Renos K. Papadopoulos (Ed.), *Therapeutic care for refugees: No place like home* (pp. 57–68). The Tavistock Clinic Series. Karnac.

Friedman, M., & Jaranson, J. (1994). The applicability of the posttraumatic stress disorder concept to refugees. In A. J. Marsella, T. Bornemann, S. Ekbald & J. Orely (Eds.), *Amidst peril and pain. The mental health and well-being of the world's refugees* (pp. 207–227). Washington, DC: American Psychological Association.

Jaranson, J. M. (1998). The science and politics of rehabilitating torture survivors: An overview. In J. M. Jaranson, & M. K. Popkin (Eds.), *Caring for victims of torture.* Washington, DC: American Psychiatric Press.

Marsella, A. J. (1988). Cross-cultural research on severe mental disorder: Issues and findings. *Acta Psychiatrica Scandinavica Supplementum, 344,* 7–22.

Martin-Baro, I. (1989, January 17). *The psychological consequences of political terrorism.* Transcription of the presentation made at the Symposium on the Psychological Consequences of Political Terrorism, Berkeley, California (CHRICA, Committee for Health Rights in Central America. CHRICA Mental Health Committee, 347 Dolores St., San Francisco, CA 94110).

Mehraby, N. (2002a, May). Counselling Afghanistan torture and trauma survivors. *Psychotherapy in Australia, 8,* 3.

Mehraby, N. (2002b, August). Unaccompanied child refugees: A group experience. *Psychotherapy in Australia, 8,* 4.

Orlandi, M. A. (1992). The challenge of evaluating community-based prevention programs: A cross-cultural perspective. In M. A. Orlandi (Ed.), *Cultural competence for evaluators: A guide for alcohol and other drug abuse prevention practitioners working with ethnic/racial communities.* Rockville, MD: Office for Substance Abuse Prevention.

Silove, D. (2002). The asylum debacle in Australia: A challenge for psychiatry. *Australian and New Zealand Journal of Psychiatry, 36,* 290–296.

Silove, D., & Ekblad, S. (2002). How well do refugees adapt after resettlement in Western countries? (Editorial). *Acta Psychiatrica Scandinavica, 106,* 401–402.

Steel, Z. (2001). Beyond PTSD: Towards a more adequate understanding of the multiple effects of complex trauma. In C. Moser, D. Nyfeler, & M. Verwey (Eds.). *Traumatiserungen von Flüchtlingen und Asyl Schenden: Einflus des politischen, sozialen und medizinischen Kontextes* (pp. 66–84). Zürich: Seismo.

United Nations High Commissioner for Refugees (UNHCR). (2000, November 9). *The state of the world's refugees 2000. Fifty years of humanitarian action.* United Nations High Commissioner for Refugees, Oxford University Press. Retrieved June 6, 2003, from http://www.unhcr.ch/pubs/sowr2000/sowr2000toc.htm.

van der Veer, G. (1993). *Psychotherapy with refugees. An exploration.* Amsterdam: SCS Stichting voor Culturele Studies.

Wilson, J. P. (1989) *Trauma, transformation and healing.* New York: Brunner/Mazel.

5

Assessing PTSD and Comorbidity: Issues in Differential Diagnosis

ALEXANDER C. MCFARLANE

Refugees and asylum seekers evoke images that are filled with the anguish of exile and loss. Iconic photographs and television footage convey this suffering regularly to an often unresponsive audience (Ignatieff, 1998). The challenge for the clinician is to establish whether the distress and suffering of an individual is the expected normal response in the circumstances or whether the individual has developed a psychological disorder, triggered by the trauma and dislocation he or she has endured. There is an inevitable tension between these two perspectives. Concepts such as posttraumatic stress disorder (PTSD) can be seen by activists as a language that diminishes the core political and social dilemmas at the heart of creating refugees. Recent wars such as the one in Kosovo have seen the creation of refugee populations as a primary tool of combat, to clog the roads for the movement of military forces and the imperative for the troops to tend to the humanitarian needs of the populations on the move (Ignatieff, 2001). The focus on individual pathology has the potential to hide the political and social reality of these and other tactics of repression, according to the critics (Summerfield, 1997).

Introducing the notion of illness in this setting creates anxiety that the humanity and reality of the refugees experience is diminished (Watters, 2001). Yet the failure to diagnose and treat a psychological disorder in this setting is likely to significantly add to the burden of the individual trying to adapt to extremely difficult circumstances. To deny the reality of psychological disorders in this setting can play into much of the stigma associated with mental illness in our community. The debate about labeling and the medicalization of distress in other settings have been, in part, the intellectual roots of this argument. However, veteran populations have long advocated that their rights are better served by an accurate acknowledgment and understanding of their distress (Kulka et al., 1990). Refugees are equally the victims of war and deserve the understanding and entitlements that this perspective brings within legislative and legal backgrounds.

This chapter will propose that there is a value to the careful assessment and diagnosis of refugees and asylum seekers. This approach allows the documentation and exploration of the nature and aetiology of their distress. From a practical perspective, the difficulty of assessing individuals across the barriers of language and culture will be outlined. The diagnostic category that has particular utility in this domain is PTSD. As a disorder, it encapsulates the way in which traumatic experience drives the individual's focus and preoccupation in the present, trapping the individual in the recurring suffering of the past. By its name, PTSD ties an individual's suffering to a particular experience in his or her life. In some regards, by focusing attention to an experience or event, it advocates for the restoration of rights of the individual who has been injured through social and political injustice. However, many refugees suffer from other disorders such as depression, and the task is to understand the connection between these other disorders and the traumatic experiences from the country of origin as well as to the postmigration difficulties that are inherent in the experience of being a refugee.

One of the major challenges in using a diagnosis in traumatized populations is to reflect the role of the external event while at the same time addressing the contribution of other aetiological factors that can predispose, trigger, and maintain the disorder. The increasing focus on phenomenological diagnosis in the past two decades has moved psychiatric thinking away from the notion of reactive disorders. Traumatized populations confront the simplistic separation of distress and disorder. The conceptual struggle that psychiatric classification has been through in arriving at the current formulation will be outlined. The inherent theoretical perspectives require articulation to understand the tensions that exist about using diagnosis in this setting.

Dealing with the cooccurrence of psychiatric disorders demands consideration of the issue of comorbidity. The various ways of conceptualizing comorbidity will be outlined. The scientific literature that has explored these issues specifically within the refugee population will be discussed. It should be noted that this question has been extensively examined in other traumatized populations such as veterans and general population epidemiological samples (McFarlane, 2001). Although there are specific issues relating to these matters within the refugee population, many of the principles and issues that influence comorbidity will be those that operate independent of the population being examined.

THE VALUE OF DIAGNOSIS

There are few predicaments that evoke greater humanity than that of refugees and asylum seekers. For clinicians there are few situations that are more challenging than the assessment of the individual caught in the midst of a life-and-death struggle for survival. Our concepts of psychopathology are based on observations of people embedded within societies, even if those individuals are disenfranchised as a consequence of the mental illness. The psychodynamic approach is a methodology that has a long history, where the key is the documentation of the current disturbances along a range of dimensions. This perspective implies that psychological symptoms are not solely driven by some underlying disorganization of brain function but rather reflect a reactive constellation of emotion, cognitive pattern, and behavior. This dynamic approach has a significant degree of tension with the more disease-orientated basis of the phenomenological perspective. This system is derived from the descriptive tradition of taxonomy that dominated biological and medical science in the 19th century. The latter has been criticized in anthropological and sociological circles as being reductionistic and excessively wedded to the medical model. An underlying concern revolves around the fear that people can be labeled with diagnoses of humanity, and the multidimensional nature of their experience can be lost.

These approaches are not mutually exclusive. In fact, this study of traumatic stress is the current mainstream carrier of combining the phenomenological and dynamic traditions in 21st-century psychiatry. The diagnosis of PTSD requires that the individual to be satisfied must be defined by criteria. However, the clinician has to carefully understand and dissect the nature of the individual's memory and how the content drives his or her reactivity to the current environment. For example, one reexperiencing phenomenon is increased reactivity on exposure to triggers that can be real or symbolic to the traumatic memory. A frequent cause of diagnostic error is the insensitivity of clinicians in identifying the traumatic triggers because of the subtlety of the link between the current cue and the traumatic memory. Frequently, the traumatized individual does not make a link between the current distress and some phenomenon in the environment. These triggers are often somatosensory phenomena such as smells or kinesthetic sensations. The challenge for the clinician is to identify the template that links the traumatic experience and the individual's current environment. This requires a careful and empathic engagement with the

individual's experience, both past and present. Rather than dehuman-
izing the individual suffering, it characterizes the haunting nature of
the traumatic memory and its capacity to disrupt an individual's ability
to engage with the current environment.

Avoidance of traumatic triggers similarly demands careful and subtle
analyses of the refugees' experiences. These people are often dealing
with strange and new environments, and the difficulties they have nego-
tiating these novelties can be dismissed on the basis of the unfamiliarity.
However, the fear generated can be tied to intimidation and repression
previously endured and how this threat is mirrored in the current environment. Hence, the application of this diagnostic approach requires a
dynamic assessment of how the person's current difficulties can be conceptualized on the basis of the trauma that has been inflicted upon
them. Equally, the diagnostic approach implies the development of a
treatment plan that assists in the development of a greater sense of mastery of the person's current world. There are a few other disorders that
demand the clinician to enter so carefully into the nature of the
individual's experience if the refugee is to be properly treated and diagnosed. Diagnosing a disorder does not negate the importance of addressing the practical and social needs of refugees.

PRACTICAL ISSUES OF DIAGNOSIS

Working with people from another culture is often demanding. There
are numerous barriers that complicate the process of assessment. First,
there is often the barrier of language. Diagnosis is a subtle process that
depends upon the careful use of words and the subtle nuance of understanding. Interpreters are often a necessity in the setting of interviewing
newly arrived refugees. Although experienced interpreters are of great
value, sometimes the intention of a question can be lost in translation.
Explanation to the interpreter as well as the statement of a specific
question can refine the process of phenomenological definition. It
should not be presumed that the words for emotion are directly trans-
latable. Some training of translators can assist in the refinement of the
assessment process as this can sensitize them to the nuances of language
necessary for understanding the world of emotional suffering and fear.

Within the specific diagnostic criteria there are multiple layers of
understanding that have to be dissected. For example, avoidance is a
process and behavior that can take many forms. An individual who has
been tortured might choose an extremely restricted lifestyle devoid of
many possible experiences because this prevents a confrontation with
the process of choice that presented impossible conundrums. Torture
often presents impossible choices to an individual where any action
leads to punishment. With freedom, any choice presents the reminder
of punishment and therefore threatens. To prevent this possibility,
avoiding choice becomes the primary driver of behavior. The subtleties

of this pattern are often not directly recognized by the patient. To recognize the significance of such a behavior demands a particular sensitivity on the part of the clinician. Such restrictions in an individual's life might not be reported if a direct question is asked about avoidance since the significance cannot be understood.

Respect for the beliefs and value systems is a given in understanding the histories of refugees and asylum seekers. As an outsider to a culture there are two conflicting demands. One is to presume that their existence is exotic and demands a unique lens of understanding. In some regards, the anthropological specificities of cultures demand these sensitivities. On the other hand, there are considerable diversities within a culture particularly in the attitudes to the effects of trauma. One has only to compare the differences between the attitudes in the military with those in the women's movement to realize the polarities and diversities that can exist within a culture. It is therefore important not to presume but to observe with each patient the values of their world. After studying psychiatric disorder following an earthquake in the poorest province of China in 1989 (Cao, McFarlane, & Klimidis, 2003) and having heard the histories of over 1,000 patients in Kuwait presented by medical students, the similarities of humanity, independent of culture, should equally not be ignored. People from different cultures can evoke a sense of the exotic and difference. However, it is equally important not to be dazzled by the differences and to remember that there are universalities that drive the dimensions of human distress that have their origins in our biological evolutionary roots.

The observation, understanding, and assessment of people should be informed but not excessively by precise diagnostic systems. Currently both ICD-10 (WHO, 1992) and DSM-IV (American Psychiatric Association, 1996) are systems that have currency in the international literature. The thresholds for the diagnosis of PTSD are significantly higher using the DSM-IV criteria, with ICD-10 giving nearly three times more cases in epidemiological samples (Creamer, Burgess, & McFarlane, 2001; Peters, Slade, & Andrews, 1999). The difference between these systems suggests that there are many issues about the clinical characterization of the reactions to trauma requiring clarification than the current literature would suggest (see Table 5.1). The process of publication demands the use of internationally defined systems of diagnosis, which can inhibit the exploration of the subtleties of phenomenology in culturally distinct samples. Hence, clinicians should not be averse to noting the contradictions and subtle inconsistencies that are observed with patients. These phenomena should be considered and addressed in the treatment of patients. The impact that the extremes of torture and persecution can have on personality functioning is also an issue that should be assessed. ICD-10 recognizes the capacity for such experiences to lead to specific personality pathology as indicated by the category enduring personality change after catastrophic experience (WHO, 1992). This category should be considered when an individual presents a pervasive sense of

TABLE 5.1 Comparison Between ICD-10 DCR and DSM-IV PTSD

ICD-10 DCR	DSM-IV
A. Exposure to stressor	A1. Exposure to stressor
	A2. Emotional reaction to stressor
B. Persistent remembering of the stressor in one of following ways: intrusive flashbacks, vivid memories or recurring dreams, experiencing distress when reminded of the stressor.	B. Traumatic event reexperienced in one or more of the following ways:
	B1. Intrusive recollections
	B2. Distressing dreams
	B3. Acting/feeling as though the event were recurring
	B4. Psychological distress when exposed to reminders
	B5. Physiological reactivity when exposed to reminders
C. Requires actual or preferred avoidance of circumstances resembling or associated with the stressor.	C. Requires avoidance of stimuli associated with trauma and numbing of general responsiveness as indicated by three (or more) of the following:
	C1. Avoidance of thoughts, feelings, or conversations associated with stressor
	C2. Avoidance of activities, places, or people associated with the stressor
	C3. Inability to recall important aspects of trauma
	C4. Diminished interest and participation in significant activities
	C5. Feeling of detachment from others
	C6. Restricted range of affect
	C7. Sense of foreshortened future

TABLE 5.1 continued

ICD-10 DCR	DSM-IV
Either D1 or D2	D. Persistent symptoms of increased arousal as indicated by two (or more) of the following:
D1. Inability to recall some important aspects of period of exposure to the stressor	
D2. Persistent symptoms of increased physiological arousal as shown by any two of the following:	D1. Sleep problems
	D2. Irritability or outbursts of anger
	D3. Concentration problems
sleep problems	D4. Hypervigilance
irritability	D5. Exaggerated startle response
concentration problems	
hypervigilance	
exaggerated startle response	
E. Onset of symptoms within 6 months of the stressor.	E. Duration of disturbance at least 1 month.
	F. Disturbance causes clinically significant distress or impairment in social, occupational, or other important functioning.

Source: Adapted from Peters, L., Slade, T., & Andrews, G. (1999).

vigilance, distrust, feelings of emptiness, and defensive aggression as an alternative to a diagnosis of a paranoid disorder. Making these differentiations from more longstanding personality pathology can be difficult. Political dissidents are, by the nature of their willingness to take risks and stand up against repressive regimes, not ordinary people.

The challenge of research and structured diagnostic instruments poses a different set of questions and challenges. Interest exists in being able to contrast and compare populations from different cultural and ethnic populations. Although there are gains possible from being able to use the same instrument across populations, the specificities of response in individuals will be lost. The growth of the international research community and epidemiology has led to many studies that have aimed to define the prevalence of psychiatric disorders in many countries that have been inflicted with war and disasters and have resulted in people fleeing those nations. Many such studies have not yet entered the domain of the international literature but include Kuwait, Lebanon, Palestine, Iran, and Sri Lanka that have used WHO's Composite International Diagnostic Interview (CIDI) (Andrews & Peters, 1998). The benefit of such instruments is that comparisons can occur between diverse settings and with individuals who have been resettled from the areas of conflicts and terrorism. The CIDI is a structured diagnostic interview that can be administered by lay interviewers.

In clinical settings there is often a need to use self-report questionnaires. Many have been used in cross-cultural settings. It is essential that translation and then back translation be used to ensure the accuracy and applicability of the language. The Harvard Trauma Questionnaire is one instrument that has been used widely in refugee populations and whose facility has been widely demonstrated (Mollica et al., 1992). Also measures such as the PTSD Checklist (PCL) and the Impact of Events–Revised (IES-R) (Asukai et al., 2002) have equally been utilized in many different cultural settings with disaster and refugee populations. Currently, the practice is to use questionnaires translated from English that have been developed in Western cultures.

REACTIVE DISTRESS OR ESTABLISHED DISORDER?

Historically, psychiatric classification has struggled with the diagnosis and conceptualization of acute reactions to stress (McFarlane, 2003). Particularly when the individual remains in an environment were there is an ongoing threat, the challenge is the separation of pathological responses to those that are normal states of mind. At one level, this requires the separation of normal fear from panic or dissociation in a situation where a person can fear for his or her life. Alternatively, if a person is faced with loss, the dilemma emerges as to the difference and the similarity between grief and depression. With refugee populations this can pose a particular problem because it can be very difficult to define when an individual's traumatic experience has ended. In the first instance, asylum seekers and refugees will have had to cope with persecution and threat in their country of origin. They then are likely to have endured prolonged periods in refugee camps where they will have faced privations, threats due to the civil disorganization, boredom, and the continual reminders of what they have lost. On arriving in the country of asylum, language, cultural, and discrimination issues will continue to take their toll. When faced with acute threat, an individual manages in a survival mode (Chemtob et al., 1999). This state of mind is characterized by vigilance to the external environment, an imperative to respond to threat with action; a relative insensitivity to one's emotional needs for comfort; and a narrow temporal focus.

It is only when individuals feel safe that they can begin to relax and take stock of what they have experienced. This involves contemplation and reflection with the present being placed in a longer historical context of the person's life. The meaning of what has happened and the search for explanations begin in this setting. The greater degree of introspection at this time can precipitate the emergence of distress as the loss and threat is processed. In trying to understand the individual's state of adaptation, it is necessary to contemplate whether the individual is still in a survival mode or whether they have moved into a state of long-term adaptation. This concept is imbedded in the notion of PTSD. The name implies that this is a state that occurs in the aftermath of traumatic experience and should be separated from the individual's reaction at the time of the trauma. The challenge then comes as to how to conceptualize and understand the different states that can affect individuals when they are trapped in a world of ongoing danger, uncertainty, and loss. A clinician has to enter these dimensions to consider a patient's experience from an empathic perspective.

Most psychiatric disorders do not demand the clinician to carefully consider the issue of context. Rather, the diagnosis depends upon the careful description and elucidation of the individual's current symptoms and the stand independent of the individual's current experience. For example, in schizophrenia, the presence of hallucinations and delusions is defined independently of any interpersonal or environment crises. In fact, current psychiatric nomenclature has moved away from the notion of reactive disorders. Categories such as a reactive depression no longer exist. Independent of the course, a diagnosis of major depressive disorder is made. The criticisms raised against this approach are based on the fear that normal distress is being labeled as psychopathology. The counter to the line of argument is that psychiatric disorders are known to emerge in settings of stress and therefore likely to exist with greater prevalence in stressed individuals. Dismissing the individual's reaction as a normal response can deny that person the benefits of treatment.

The most detailed analysis of these issues emerges from the experience of military psychiatry. The critical challenge has been the development of a method of understanding and managing the acute breakdown of soldiers in combat. In part the conceptualization of this problem has emerged from the careful observation and clinical experience of those involved (Solomon, Laor, & McFarlane, 1996). Social pressures and pragmatic issues have impinged on the military formulation of how to deal with soldiers who break down in battle (Shepard, 2001). The military establishment has realized that the behavioral disorganization of soldiers in combat is not simply due to cowardice and lack of moral fiber. In this regard, a medical diagnosis has protected soldiers from disciplinary action and humiliation. Equally, there has been significant pressure placed on the medical corps to minimize the number of psychological casualties because of the importance of maintaining the fighting force. Psychiatrists have been criticized for too readily moving soldiers from the front, a decision that has often been welcomed by the soldier who then avoids the risks of future combat (Shepard, 2001). There was also concern that soldiers became chronically disabled because of the expectation of prolonged dysfunction. This apprehension was reinforced because of the secondary gains from being ill. To counter the perceived problems caused by evacuation from the front, the practice of forward psychiatry was introduced.

There are four key elements to this approach (Glass, 1974). First, the services should be provided as close as possible to the fighting unit from which the individual came: proximity. Second, the treatment should be provided as rapidly as possible following the disruption of the individual's capacity to cope: immediacy. This approach minimizes the potential of the problem becoming entrenched. At the time of presentation there was minimal diagnostic exploration and characterization of symptoms. Third, there was the communication to the patient that his or her behavior was an understandable response to the circumstances of extreme combat, and there was the anticipation that one would greatly recover since he or she was now in a situation of safety and response: expectancy. In other words, there was an attempt to minimize the transition or the inducements to take on the sick role. Fourth, the intervention had minimal exploration of the individual's beliefs and feelings about his or her experience. The approach focused on rest, reassurance, and anticipation of recovery: simplicity. Exploratory psychotherapy was actively discouraged. The system was established to return the soldier to his or her combat role as soon as possible. Conceptually, practice had moved from seeing these individuals as having a disorder to having a transitory reaction to extreme stress.

This conceptualization and the practice of it for psychiatry captured the interest of many mental health professionals, particularly during World War II. The emphasis had also moved from the individual to the role of leaders in maintaining group cohesion because of the protective effect this could have on soldiers when faced with extreme stress. Social psychiatry and crisis theory emerged from this setting (Raphael, 1977). The success that these interventions had in the military setting prompted optimism about short-term and crisis-focused interventions in civilian practice. Grief counseling, disaster psychiatry, and cross intervention were directly derived from the military environment (Raphael, 1977). Much of the modern practice of community psychiatry is also an adaptation of the notions of proximity and expectancy. Although the benefits of this approach were demonstrated by the decrease in the number of chronic combat casualties, this is also a system that can be subject to misapplication. In one sense, the needs of the individual are placed as second to the needs of the group. The system is structured to minimize the rates of diagnosis and the number of individuals who require more in-depth and substantial treatment. In a refugee population, the desire to prevent stigmatization by diagnosis can inadvertently lead to the minimizing of a significant injury.

A second, and unforeseen, consequence of this approach and its success was the failure to understand the nature of chronic posttraumatic reactions. It was believed that once the stress had ceased, the individual's symptoms would be resolved. The logical result was the failure to understand how stress could affect individuals in the long term. It was presumed that individuals who did not break down at the time of their exposure were immune to the long-term consequences of their trauma. If they broke down during their lifetime, it was attributed to predisposition and vulnerability factors. The dominance of the psychoanalytic model of psychopathology conceptualized these latter symptoms as being due to unresolved developmental conflicts (Glass, 1974). There was a failure to understand how extreme stress in adult life could have long-term and disabling effects on some individuals. PTSD emerged out of the recognition that the majority of individuals who broke down following combat had coped satisfactorily at the time. The danger for refugees is that if a paradigm of reactive psychopathology is used exclusively, there will be a failure to understand the long-term scars they bare for their persecution and exile.

These issues are outlined because it is presumed that medical diagnosis can disempower individuals and stigmatize them. Some activists are therefore reluctant about the use of psychopathological concepts to describe refugees and asylum seekers, believing this can distract from the political reality and social prejudice they face. In other words, medical diagnosis is seen to undermine the reality of these people's suffering and the need for social intervention. The experience of war veterans demonstrates the reverse, namely, that social systems can conspire to deny the existence of psychological injury because it demands accountability of those responsible. In the military if individuals could be blamed as being weak and vulnerable, it was not a matter for the commanders. Once the responsibility of the environment and the group were expected as critical to the rates of combat stress disorder, steps were taken to better protect service personnel. In any political debate, there is a powerful valence if you can argue that an individual's health is damaged through the acts of third parties. Rather than disenfranchising the welfare of refugees and asylum seekers, the demonstration of psychological injury can be a powerful political argument. In the recent debate in Australia over asylum seekers, the media has given considerable attention to the demonstrated rates of psychiatric disorder in these people. It has also opened avenues of legal recourse against the government and its instrumentalities, which would otherwise been denied.

Therefore, the diagnostic assessment of refugees and asylum seekers demands careful attention to both their current life experiences and the traumatic environment from which they have come. The characteristics and components of these different time epochs have to be carefully assessed if an individual is to be appropriately diagnosed. The diagnosis is not to negate the terrible experiences and political disenfranchisement that characterize these people's lives. Rather, it can empower them by giving them recourse through the legal system as well as in shoring down and not being left with the burden of untreated illness. The last thing that an individual needs when trying to cope with the adaptation of demands of settling in a new country is the loss of motivation, the withdrawal, and the negativity associated with depression.

DISORDERS SECONDARY TO STRESS

PTSD represented a major departure from the other diagnostic categories in DSM-III because it assumed the primary etiological role of the traumatic event in this disorder. Unlike past diagnostic systems, DSM-III (American Psychiatric Association, 1980) took an atheoretical position in relation to etiology, and PTSD represented an important exception to the general rule because the etiological agent was included in the diagnosis. Encapsulated within the diagnostic criteria for PTSD are the three sets of symptomatic response: the reexperiencing of the trauma, the avoidance and numbing, and hyperarousal. One major criticism of this formulation is that it has been universally accepted with little examination of the cross-cultural validity. The analysis of distinct data sets has demonstrated the critical role of the traumatic reexperiencing phenomenon in leading to the onset of the avoidance and hyperarousal symptoms of this condition. This observation is in keeping with the theoretical role of the traumatic memory in leading to the neurobiological dysregulation that is a core of PTSD (Vermetten & Bremner, 2002). Equally, it accounts for the conditioning process that underlies the hyperresponsiveness to the range of traumatic triggers that dominate and influence the life of the individual with this disorder (Pitman et al., 1993).

Until recently, PTSD has been accepted as the main disorder that begins in the aftermath of traumatic events (Breslau, 1998). However, it has been recognized that a range of other disorders such as depression, panic disorder, and a generalized anxiety disorder occur not infrequently (McFarlane & Papay, 1992). Shalev et al. (1998), for example, found that 29% of those with major depression did not have comorbid PTSD and concluded that major depression and PTSD are independent sequelae of traumatic events. Similarly, Schnyder et al. (2001), in a sample of severely injured accident victims, reported that nearly 20% suffered from depression and/or anxiety independent of PTSD at 12 months posttrauma. If these existed in the absence of PTSD, the question arises as to what relationship their onset has to the experience of the traumatic event. In particular, many of these individuals described the same reexperience in principle but did not satisfy the full diagnostic criteria for PTSD (McFarlane, 1992). This observation has led to an increasing interest as to whether the traumatic exposure plays an important role in the onset of these disorders or whether the disorders emerge as a consequence of other vulnerabilities and intercurrent stresses in the individual's life. Although the evidence suggests that the link to the trauma is perhaps not as direct as with PTSD, the traumatic memory in a significant proportion of cases appears to play an important role in driving the symptoms.

Just as severe threat and the confrontation with horror are critical to the development of PTSD, it has long been postulated that loss is a central emotion in the etiology of depression (Tennant, 1983). Progressively there has been decreasing interest in this notion because it has its roots in psychodynamic thinking. Brown, Harris, and Eales (1996) have continued to investigate the interaction between adversity in different time frames and have shown that the rate of anxiety and depression was highly related to childhood experiences of neglect and abuse. However, adversity in adult life was only related to the rate of depression, not anxiety.

In the area of PTSD, the interaction between the nature of the traumatic exposure and cormorbidity has received little attention. In a study of Vietnam veterans, panic disorder with PTSD is related to the severity of combat exposure (Green, Lindy, Grace, & Gleser, 1989). In a study of disaster victims, the interaction between the losses sustained and the intensity of personal threat can be impacted by the life events an individual experienced both prior to and after the trauma. McFarlane and Papay (1992) found that anxiety and depression were influenced by adversity before and after, whereas PTSD is associated with higher exposure. These findings provide some support for the model where specific types of stressors impact on the coexistence of PTSD, and other disorders have been an issue of interest in populations who have faced multiple adversities.

These relationships have been looked at in detail in one study of Turkish torture survivors (Basoglu, Paker, Ozmen, Tasdemir, & Sahin, 1994). Although those studied were not refugees, these data can inform the impact of political abuse and dislocation on refugees. Three types of stressors were documented and their relationship to different aspects of psychopathology in survivors of torture were investigated, namely, perceived severity of torture, secondary effects of captivity experience on various life areas, and general psychosocial stressors following captivity. The perceived severity of torture was related to PTSD symptoms but not to anxiety or depression. Lack of social support predicted anxiety and depression but not PTSD. Impact of captivity experience on family was the strongest predictor of PTSD symptoms. However, this could in part be due to the PTSD symptoms of the torture victim.

Although the broader context and experience of a refugee should be assessed, the primacy of their traumatic exposures should not be underestimated as the driver of their chronic distress. Steel et al. (2002), in a long-term research of Vietnamese refugees in Australia, found a pattern where traumatic exposure was the most consistent predictor of morbidity. In contrast, Miller et al. (2002), in a study of recent Bosnian refugees, found that PTSD was associated with the levels of trauma and this also predicted social isolation. Depression was primarily accounted for by the exile-related stressors as well as the role of war-related stresses.

Thus, there is a body of research indicating the need to better understand the role of the various dimensions of the refugee experience and the range of disorders that are observed in these people. In particular, the multiplicity of adversities has been used as one explanation for the existence of comorbidity in association with PTSD. From a diagnosis point of view, the implications of comorbidity in refugee populations requires consideration because of its implications for the etiology, treatment, and prognosis of an individual's distress.

COMORBIDITY

In refugee populations where depression is a frequent phenomenon, the best way to conceptualize and manage these reactions has obvious clinical and theoretical importance. The conceptual problem relates to the existence of symptoms within a traumatized population that are not described by PTSD. Up until DSM-IIIR (American Psychiatric Association, 1987) it was accepted that there was a hierarchy of diagnosis where a single diagnosis was preferable. When a disorder at the top of the hierarchy was diagnosed, all other disorders would be subsumed under that diagnosis. Thus, anxiety disorders would be subsumed under a diagnosis of a depressive disorder. This was in keeping with the general practice of parsimony of medical diagnosis that presumes one explanation will be a sorting factor for multiple symptoms. DSM-III (1980) accepted this hierarchical system but this was modified in the light of DSM-IIIR (1987). This practice was changed in the light of evidence the unexpected frequency of the cooccurrence of symptom clusters using the more systematic diagnostic approach that DSM-III had brought to psychiatry.

This coexistence of disorders became apparent because the development of structured diagnostic interviews that were routinely applied in epidemiological and clinical samples indicated that the full criteria for a number of disorders were met within a given individual. Previous clinical practice, prior to the use of such structured interviews and operationalized diagnostic criteria, did not encourage the exhaustive assessment of a patient's mental state. This prevented recognition of the multiplicity of symptoms that would often occur within the same individual.

Feinstein (1970) first coined the term comorbidity to address the observation that the outcome of clinical trials in medicine often varied when disorders other than those under study were present. Comorbidity was defined as any distinct additional clinical entity occurring during the clinical course of a patient who had the index disorder under study. These disorders had the potential to influence the detection, prognosis, and treatment response. However, comorbidity remains poorly defined and lacks clear conceptualization (Maser & Cloninger, 1990). In particular it is unclear whether the disorders must be contemporaneously present across a defined period of time (Andrews, 1996). Comorbidity specifically refers to the existence of multiple disorders within a given individual. The challenge was how to explain the multiplicity of disorders.

There are a series of competing explanations about the mechanism of comorbidity:

1. The Psychodynamic Model. This proposes, as outlined above, that the matrix of antecedent events and those that follow a traumatic event will influence the pattern of disorders that emerge, above and beyond PTSD. Furthermore, the degrees of fear, helplessness, and horror experienced during the traumatic event can influence the patterns of comorbidity.
2. Complication Model. According to this formulation PTSD acts as a stressor that leads to a secondary disorder such as depression. According to this model, the number of comorbid disorders will directly relate to the severity of the PTSD.
3. Predispositional Model. Prior psychiatric disorder is recognized as a predisposing factor for PTSD and hence depression could predispose to PTSD and conversely, PTSD could lead to a disregulation of the underlying biological modulators of mood.
4. Common Diathesis Model. The vulnerability factors for PTSD such as neuroticism and poor social support can also predispose an individual to the onset of another disorder on exposure to the trauma. In this model, the two disorders are conceptually independent of each other.
5. Form Fruste Model. In this model disorders such as generalized anxiety disorder can represent a subsyndromal disorder where the primary disorder in a subclinical form would account for many of the symptoms.
6. Interactional Model. Two disorders when they coexist can serve to magnify the severity of the other. For example, the presence of a borderline personality disorder will both increase the symptoms of a PTSD due to inability to regulate the distress associated with the traumatic memories and be worsened by the emotional disregulation that accompanies PTSD.

Some of these models conceptually overlap, and more than one model can apply to a given set of comorbid disorders. In relation to PTSD, the issue of comorbidity has tended to follow the convention where it is presumed that the PTSD is the primary condition and the other disorders assume secondary significance. This largely unspoken convention presumes that the traumatic memory structure that is critical to the etiological process in PTSD (Pitman et al., 1993), leads to a secondary disregulation of affect or anxiety, being manifest as a major depressive disorder and panic disorder, for example. The question is far from clear where the reverse circumstances arise. In particular, if an individual becomes depressed following a traumatic life event and then develops a secondary PTSD, there is not the same acceptance of the primary etiological role of the traumatic stressor. Furthermore, in such cases, one should not presume that the treatments that address the traumatic stress will be effective in treating the primary disorder. In such cases, the treatments defined in the literature for that primary disorder would be seen to be the clinically appropriate steps to implement. In assessing refugees these various possibilities require careful consideration because of the need to take a longitudinal perspective of the many stresses that have been experienced and their potential interaction with the range of disorders experienced by the individual. Pejovic and Jovanovic (1996) showed that there might also be specific effects influencing comorbidity in victims of the same war when comparing refugees and war veterans in Serbia. They found that the clinical picture of depression in refugees was the hopelessness that losses caused by exile, war, and veterans' depression was a severe and chronic complication of PTSD.

Thus, addressing the issue of comorbidity in refugees requires sensitivity both to the reactive nature of the range of symptoms and the impact of specific stressors, as well as the possibility that comorbid disorders could have their origins in some of the associated mechanisms described above. In particular, associated disorders can be markers of particular predispositions to a disorder or a consequence of the severity of the PTSD. Clearly, weighing the possibilities is important in designing a treatment program where both the individuals' experiences and their vulnerabilities should be given due consideration. Lie (2002) has demonstrated that despite the restitution of a degree of social stability, symptoms remained and highlighted the need to provide treatment for psychological disorders and that addressing psychosocial adversity in itself will not resolve the significant disadvantage that PTSD brings.

PATTERNS OF SYMPTOM PRESENTATION IN REFUGEES

Somatic Symptoms

One of the most challenging aspects of dealing with trauma victims is the clinical problem that somatic complaints such as weakness, lethargy, headaches, abdominal pain, and neck and back pain are the primary presentation. Burnett and Peel (2001), in a study of refugees in the United Kingdom, found infrequently that these symptoms had a physical basis, despite the fervently held conviction of the patients. This was despite the fact that the patients themselves often recognized the interrelationship between physical and psychological symptoms. These presentations are demanding because major clinical improvement is difficult to achieve. Again it should be recognized that somatic complaints are common in PTSD, independent of the cultural background. In veterans' populations, the controversy surrounding Agent Orange and the Gulf War syndrome are two examples of the same tensions that exist between clinicians and traumatized patients.

Van Ommeren et al. (2002) examined the relative contribution of PTSD against anxiety and depression as the determinant of physical symptoms in Bhutanese refugees. They found that the number of PTSD symptoms, and not depression and anxiety, predicted both the number of reported somatic complaints and the number of organ systems reflected in these complaints. These somatic symptoms are often a major focus of complaint and disability in refugee populations, and their management represents a major challenge.

Disability and Comorbidity

Mollica et al. (1999) examined the relationship between disability, psychological symptoms, and health status. They found a significant association as would be expected between perceived health status, psychological symptoms, and disability. PTSD and depression particularly predicted high levels of disability. These findings encapsulate the predicament of dealing with comorbidities in refugee populations because highly sophisticated clinical interventions are necessary with such presentations. The limitations of language and culture make affective interventions for these presentations very challenging. Furthermore, the careful exclusion of underlying organic pathology can be hampered because of the language barrier.

Other barriers to care exist within refugee populations. One is the extent to which these atypical clinical presentations are influenced by comorbidity and severity of disorder. Weine et al. (2000) concluded that those who do not seek services still had significant symptom levels compared with those seeking treatment. However, their self-concept appears to be less oriented toward illness and help-seeking, emphasizing the need for innovative access, engagement, and preventive interventions needed to address those who have symptoms but do not readily seek help for trauma mental health services.

Organic Brain Injury

Weinstein, Razzano, and Millica (2001) have cautioned clinicians in dealing with refugee populations to consider the background nutritional and physical traumas that have been suffered in a diagnostic assessment. In particular, a range of psychiatric symptoms can be secondary to the effect of traumatic brain injury. These findings emphasize the need to have a thorough assessment of the physical health status of refugees presenting with psychological distress. The results allow an informed educational approach to the management of the range of pathologies identified.

Cultural Specificity

There is little doubt that being a refugee brings with it a complex congregation of events. The challenge is to separate the effects of the trauma experienced in the country of origin from the stresses of migration and acculturation in a host society, which is often very different from the one that has been escaped from. From a research point of view, it is important to separate these effects of migration from the underlying experience of being a refugee. The study of a series of ethnic minorities in Sweden provided an opportunity to investigate these issues (Bayard, Sundquist, & Johansson, 2001). High rates of psychiatric illness and the use of psychotropic drugs were identified among Iranians, Chileans, Turks, and Kurds. They were compared with Polish adults also living in Sweden. The particular impact of living alone, poor acculturation, unemployment, and a low sense of social coherence were examined a decade after arriving in the country. In general, migration was associated with greater levels of psychological distress. The Chilean and Iranian populations appear to be particularly at risk, although the differences were small in contrast to the Poles. It is also important to be aware that associations and patterns of morbidity in one group of refugees might not necessarily be the case in another.

It seems there are a limited number of patterns that occur across cultures in terms of the clinical presentations in refugee populations. Beiser, Cargo, and Woodbury (1994) contrasted the phenomenology of depression among Southeast Asian refugees with resident Canadians and concluded that depressive disorders occurred across many cultures, in more or less invariant forms. There are many studies of similar observations, suggesting that there are a limited number of diatheses by which humans respond to adversity (McFarlane, 2001). The commonalities of response would appear to be greater than the differences. In dealing with refugee populations, a clinician must therefore carefully balance the exotic uniqueness of refugees and their particular social and cultural needs against the principles that he derived from the common generalities of psychopathological observation. It is important not to be distracted from the clinical reality of the depressive disorder that will respond well to treatment by focusing to an excessive degree on the psychosocial dimensions and other preoccupations of the individual's distress.

Children and Comorbidity

Children deserve specific mention because of the great potential for the disruption of their normal development by the refugee experience. Hubbard, Realmuto, Northwood, and Masten (1995) demonstrated that a range of comorbid disorders also emerge in individuals who develop PTSD as children and need to be addressed in treatment, including somatization disorder especially in females. Hodes (2000) concluded that up to 40% of these children could have psychiatric disorders, mostly depression, PTSD, and other anxiety-related difficulties. This poses a particular challenge in terms of the treatment services, which must deal with the educational, social, and mental health needs of the parents and children alike. Mghir, Freed, Raskin, and Katon (1995), in a study of Afghani refugees in their late adolescence, found a positive correlation between psychiatric diagnosis and parental level of psychological distress (especially maternal distress) above and beyond the trauma exposures. There were negative correlations between children's symptomatology and a measure of maternal acculturation. Hence, children and adolescents need to be assessed as part of a social system.

CONCLUSION

The assessment and diagnosis of refugees pose many challenges to a clinician. Although the humanistic challenge demands that the political and practical requirements of these people be dealt with, it is equally important to address their psychiatric morbidity. The barriers of language and culture present a series of practical and theoretical hurdles in this setting but can be pragmatically addressed. To leave psychiatric disorders such as depression and PTSD undiagnosed and untreated represents a considerable source of burden of suffering to the individual. The issue of comorbidity brings into focus the issue of whether the trauma of being a refugee causes particular patterns of distress driven by the immediate predicament being endured or whether the stress precipitates a specific psychiatric disorder that persists in the absence of the immediate experience. The continuing political instability of the Middle East and Africa means that humanitarian emergencies will continue to demand the attention and moral concern of Western nations in the 21st century. The diagnosis of the psychiatric morbidity of these peoples plays an important role in describing the burden and suffering that terrorism and political turmoil inflict.

References

American Psychiatric Association. (1980). *Diagnostic and statistical manual of mental disorders* (3rd ed.). Washington, DC: Author.

American Psychiatric Association. (1996). *Diagnostic and statistical manual of mental disorders* (4th ed.). Washington, DC: Author.

Andrews G. (1996). Comorbidity and the general neurotic syndrome. *British Journal of Psychiatry, 168*(suppl. 30), 76–84.

Andrews, G., & Peters, L. (1998). Psychometric properties of the CIDI. *Social Psychiatry and Psychiatric Epidemiology, 33,* 80–88.

Asukai, N., Kato, H., Kawamura, N., Kim, Y., Yamamoto, K., Kishimoto, J., et al. (2002). Reliability and validity of the Japanese-language version of the impact of event scale-revised (IES-R-J): Four studies of different traumatic events. *Journal Nervous Mental Disorders, 190,* 175–182.

Basoglu, M., Paker, M., Ozmen, E., Tasdemir, O., & Sahin, D. (1994, August 3). Factors related to long-term traumatic stress responses in survivors of torture in Turkey. *JAMA, 5,* 357–363

Bayard-Burfield, L., Sundquist, J., & Johansson, S. E. (2001). Ethnicity, self reported psychiatric illness, and intake of psychotropic drugs in five ethnic groups in Sweden. *Journal of Epidemiology and Community Health, 55*(9), 657–664.

Beiser, M., Cargo, M., & Woodbury, M. A. (1994). A comparison of psychiatric disorder in different cultures: Depressive typologies in Southeast Asian refugees and resident Canadians. *International Journal of Methods in Psychiatric Research, 4*(3), 157–172.

Breslau, N. (1998). Epidemiology of trauma and posttraumatic stress disorder. In R. Yehuda (Ed.), *Psychological trauma* (Vol. 17, pp. 1–29). Washington, DC: American Psychiatric Press.

Brown, G. W., Harris, T. O., & Eales, M. J. (1996). Social factors and comorbidity of depressive and anxiety disorders. *British Journal of Psychiatry, 168*(suppl. 30), 50–57.

Burnett, A., & Peel, M. (2001). Asylum seekers and refugees in Britain: The health of survivors of torture and organised violence. *British Medical Journal, 322*(7286), 606–609.

Cao, H., McFarlane, A. C., & Klimidis, S. (2003). Prevalence of psychiatric disorder following the 1988 Yun Nan (China) earthquake — the first 5-month period. *Social Psychiatry and Psychiatric Epidemiology, 38*(4), 204–212.

Chemtob, C. M., Roitblat, H. L., Hamada, R. S., Muraoka, M. Y., Carlson, J. G., & Bauer, G. B. (1999). Compelled attention: The effects of viewing trauma-related stimuli on concurrent task performance in posttraumatic stress disorder. *Journal of Trauma and Stress, 12,* 309–326.

Creamer, M., Burgess, P., & McFarlane, A.C. (2001). Post-traumatic stress disorder: Findings from the Australian National Survey of Mental Health and Wellbeing. *Psychological Medicine, 31*(7), 1237–1247.

Feinstein, A. R. (1970). The pre-therapeutic classification of comorbidity in chronic disease. *Journal of Chronic Diseases, 23,* 455–468.

Glass, A. J. (1974). Mental health programs in the armed services. In S. Arieti (Ed.), *American handbook of psychiatry* (pp. 800–809). New York: Basic Books.

Green, B. L., Lindy, J. D., Grace, M. C., & Gleser, G. C. (1989, June). Multiple diagnosis in posttraumatic stress disorder. The role of war stressors. *Journal of Nervous and Mental Disorder 177*(6), 329–335.

Ignatieff, M. (1998). *The warrior's honor: Ethnic war and the modern conscience.* New York: Vintage.

Ignatieff, M. (2001). *The secret war: Kosovo and beyond.* New York: Vintage.

Hodes, M. (2000). Psychological distressed refugee children in the United Kingdom. *Child Psychology and Psychiatry Review, 5*(2), 57–68.

Hubbard, J., Realmuto, G. M., Northwood, A. K., & Masten, A. S. (1995). Comorbidity of psychiatric diagnoses with posttraumatic stress disorder in survivors of childhood trauma. *Journal of the American Academy of Child and Adolescent Psychiatry, 34*(9), 1167–1173.

Kulka, R. A., Schlenger, W. E., Fairbank, J. A., Hough, R. L., Jordan, B. K., Marmar, C. R., et al. (1990). *Trauma and the Vietnam war generation: Report of the findings from the National Vietnam Veterans Readjustment Study.* New York: Brunner/Mazel.

Maser, J. D., & Cloninger, C. R. (1990). *Comorbidity of anxiety and mood disorders.* Washington DC: APP.

McFarlane, A. C. (1992). Avoidance and intrusion in posttraumatic stress disorder. *Journal of Nervous and Mental Disease, 180*(7), 439–445.

McFarlane, A. C. (2000). Ethnocultural issues. In D. Nutt, J. R. T. Davidson, & J. Zohar (Eds.), *Posttraumatic stress disorder: Diagnosis, management and treatment* (pp. 187–198). London: Martin Dunitz.

McFarlane, A. C. (2001). Dual diagnosis and treatment of PTSD. In J. Wilson, M. Friedman, & J. Lindy (Eds.), *Treating psychological trauma and PTSD* (pp. 237–254). New York: Guilford Publications, 2001.

McFarlane, A. C. (2003). Early reactions to traumatic events: The diversity of diagnostic formulations. In R. Orner, & U. Schnyder (Eds.), *Reconstructing early intervention after trauma: Innovations in the care of survivors* (pp. 237–254). New York: Oxford University Press.

McFarlane, A. C., & Papay, P. (1992). Multiple diagnoses in posttraumatic stress disorder in the victims of a natural disaster. *Journal of Nervous and Mental Disease, 180*, 498–504.

Mghir, R., Freed, W., Raskin, A., & Katon, W. (1995, January). Depression and posttraumatic stress disorder among a community sample of adolescent and young adult Afghan refugees. *Journal of Nervous and Mental Disease, 183*(1), 24–30.

Miller, K. E., Weine, S. M., Ramic, A., Brkic, N., Bjedic, Z. D., Smajkic, A., et al. (2002, October). The relative contribution of war experiences and exile-related stressors to levels of psychological distress among Bosnian refugees. *Journal of Trauma and Stress, 15*(5), 377–387.

Mollica, R. F., Caspi-Yavin, Y., Bollini, P., Truong, T., Tor, S., & Lavelle, J. (1992). The Harvard Trauma Questionnaire. Validating a cross-cultural instrument for measuring torture, trauma, and posttraumatic stress disorder in Indochinese refugees. *Journal of Nervous and Mental Disorders, 180*, 111–116.

Mollica, R. F., McInnes, K., Sarajlic, N., Lavelle, J., Sarajlic, I., & Massagli, M. P. (1999, August). Disability associated with psychiatric comorbidity and health status in Bosnian refugees living in Croatia. *JAMA, 282*(5), 433–439.

Peters, L., Slade, T., & Andrews, G. (1999). A comparison of ICD10 and DSM-IV criteria for posttraumatic stress disorder. *Journal of Traumatic Stress*, *12*(2), 335–343.

Pejovic, M., & Jovanovic, A. (1996, April–June). Depressive disorders in refugees and war veterans from Bosnia and Croatia. *Psychiatriki*, *7*(2), 124–129.

Pitman, R. K., Orr, S. P., & Shalev, A. Y. (1993). Once bitten, twice shy: Beyond the conditioning model of PTSD [editorial]. *Biological Psychiatry*, *33*(3), 145–146.

Raphael, B. (1977). Preventive intervention with the recently bereaved. *Archives of General Pyschiatry*, *34*, 1450–1454.

Schnyder, U., Moergeli, H., Trentz, O., Klaghofer, R., & Buddeberg, C. (2001). Prediction of psychiatric morbidity in severely injured accident victims at one-year follow-up. *American Journal of Respiratory & Critical Care Medicine*, *164*, 653–656.

Shalev, A. Y., Freedman, A., Peri, T., Brandes, D., Sahara, T., Orr, S., et al. (1998). Prospective study of posttraumatic stress disorder and depression following trauma. *American Journal of Psychiatry*, *155*, 630–637.

Shepard, B. (2001). *A war of nerves: Soldiers and psychiatrists in the 20th century.* Cambridge: Harvard University Press.

Solomon, Z., Laor, N., & McFarlane, A. C. (1996). Acute posttraumatic reactions in soldiers and civilians. In B. A. van der Kolk, A. C. McFarlane, & L. Weisaeth (Eds.), *Traumatic stress: The effects of overwhelming experience on mind, body and society* (pp. 102–114). New York: Guilford Publications.

Steel, Z., Silove, D., Phan, T., & Bauman, A. (2002, October). Long-term effect of psychological trauma on the mental health of Vietnamese refugees resettled in Australia: A population-based study. *Lancet*, *360*(9339), 1056–1062.

Summerfield, D. (1997). The impact of war and atrocity on civilian populations. In D. Black, M. Newman, J. Harris-Hendriks, & G. Mezey (Eds.), *Psychological trauma: A developmental approach* (pp. 148–155). London: Gaskell.

Tennant, C. (1983). Life events and psychological morbidity: The evidence from prospective studies. *Psychological Medicine*, *13*, 483–486.

Van Ommeren, M., Sharma, B., Sharma, G. K., Komproe, I., Cardena, E., & de Jong, J. T. (2002, October). The relationship between somatic and PTSD symptoms among Bhutanese refugee torture survivors: Examination of comorbidity with anxiety and depression. *Journal of Trauma and Stress*, *15*(5), 415–421.

Vermetten, E., & Bremner, J. D. (2002). Circuits and systems in stress. II. Applications to neurobiology and treatment in posttraumatic stress disorder. *Depression and Anxiety*, *16*(1), 14–38.

Watters, C. (2001, January). Emerging paradigms in the mental health care of refugees. *Social Science and Medicine*, *52*(11), 1709–1718.

Weine, S. M., Razzano, L., Brkic, N., Ramic, A., Miller, K., Smajkic, A., et al. (2000, July). Profiling the trauma related symptoms of Bosnian refugees who have not sought mental health services. *Journal of Nervous and Mental Disease*, *188*(7), 416–421.

Weinstein, C. S., Fucetola, R., & Mollica, R. (2001, September). Neuropsychological issues in the assessment of refugees and victims of mass violence. *Neuropsychology Review, 11*(3), 131–141.

World Health Organization. (1992). *The ICD-10 classification of mental and behavioural disorders clinical descriptions and diagnostic guidelines.* Geneva: Author.

Broken Spirits: Traumatic Injury to Culture, the Self, and Personality

Broken Spirits: Traumatic Injury to Culture, the Self, and Personality

Introduction

JOHN P. WILSON

Part II of the book contains two interrelated chapters. Chapter 6 by John P. Wilson examines the different ways that traumatic experiences can alter the nature of self-processes. In Chapter 7, Joop de Jong examines the inequities and complexities between health care models and the inner world of traumatization of asylum seekers and refugees. Thus, these two chapters mirror one another.

In Chapter 6, Wilson examines what it means psychologically to be a "broken spirit." Moving beyond DSM-IV conceptualizations of posttraumatic stress disorder (PTSD), the relationship of trauma and self-fragmentation is considered to rest on a continuum from extreme forms of self-fragmentation to integrative cohesion and optimal levels of functioning. The chapter includes 11 figures and 5 tables that provide visual roadmaps of the various constructs being considered.

First, Wilson's chapter begins with the important question of self-processes. What is it that constitutes the structure of the self within personality and how can it be altered by trauma and the secondary stresses of asylum seeking and becoming a waif of society as a refugee? Second, what dimensions of the self-structure are fractured by trauma, and what is their resultant adaptive configuration in personality? Third,

Wilson identifies 11 distinct posttraumatic ego processes and primary forms of psychopathology. Once having identified the different forms of self-fragmentation in personality, Wilson links these posttraumatic self-configurations to the archetypal forms of the trauma experience and the formation of the trauma complex. It is here that two new concepts are introduced, the *abyss experience* and the *inversion experience*, which respectively characterize extreme forms of trauma and the confrontation with the potential annihilation of psychic existence. Finally, Wilson illustrates how self-transformations can result in self-integration and the transformation of the trauma experience into higher forms of self-functioning.

In Chapter 7, Joop de Jong discusses public mental health and culture and looks at the relationship between disasters and their consequences for adequate health care to traumatized asylum seekers, refugees, and war and torture victims. To begin, de Jong notes that: "complex humanitarian emergencies are a challenge to our profession," which he then enumerates. Included in this sobering list is the fact that there is only one trained professional (e.g., psychiatrist, psychologist) for every 100,000 refugees among the 35 to 40 million worldwide. Next, to add to the complexity of the situation, there are relatively few resources allocated specifically to help refugees. Third, de Jong notes that in addition to insufficient resources, funding, and personnel, the refugee population requiring interventions and assistance is diverse in all relevant dimensions: language, religion, ethnicity, and assumptive beliefs and views of what is or is not considered to be mental illness and how it, in turn, should be "treated" and by whom. De Jong correctly observes that in many cultures, the role of healer is *not* that of a physician or psychologist. Traditional healers in different cultures have identifiable roles as shamans, trained healers known as *kruu*, medicine men, or other designations. He notes: "Each sort of traditional healer offers a particular target intervention ... the monks tend to focus on advice and calming people's anxieties; the *kruu*, the trained healers, provided medication and magical rituals to help rid people of invading spells and spirits and, through the public ritual, to reintegrate the person in to the local community."

To facilitate his discussion, de Jong discusses the concept of culture and the self to illustrate how culture serves to shape and influence how the person establishes an internal self-process. He argues correctly that mental health interventions must take into account the understanding of culturally molded self-processes in order to effectively know how to diagnose and treat patients suffering from trauma. De Jong concludes his chapter with suggestions that new models and paradigms should be developed for the future. These models, he suggests, should join the knowledge of the neuroscience of trauma with the anthropological wisdom of cross-cultural studies.

The Broken Spirit: Posttraumatic Damage to the Self

JOHN P. WILSON

> Weary souls displaced from their natural roots. Quietly desperate in a vacuum of loneliness. Their cries are silent. Existence in an abyss of pain and dark uncertainty. What threads remain of the past? God, who am I now?

> Wilson, 2003

ODYSSEY: TRAUMA AND ASYLUM SEEKERS, REFUGEES, WAR AND TORTURE VICTIMS

We live in a world where broken human spirits abound and surround us with their silent cries and unspoken loneliness. Torn away and uprooted from their native soil, refugees seek in desperation and mercy a safe asylum in another place where strangers live in a foreign culture with different customs, language, and histories. Asylum seekers and refugees fall into the crevices, alleys, and hallways of strange cultures and governments. They are victims and survivors of the exigencies of war, political oppression, and the insensitive foibles of corrupt, decaying, or war-torn governments. Like flotsam from a shipwreck whose debris drifts with the whims of the oceans' currents, they come to rest on the perilous shores of a strange land. Weary, desolate, and ragged from their ordeal to acquire the status of asylum seeker and refugee, they emerge tattered, exhausted, and psychically naked from the loss of their ethnic heritage and enter a new existence and way of life. Like an infant, they are passively dependent and helpless. They are at the mercy of fate and justice of bureaucratic systems that will decide whether or not they will find a safe haven or be forced to return to that life from which they sought so desperately to escape.

BROKEN SPIRITS

The regenerative powers of the ego are not limitless, the human spirit can be broken beyond repair.

Volkan, 2002, p. 2

The broken spirit is a metaphor for the fracturing of the soul, self, and identity. It is a powerful image. Malevolent forces of human design inflict injury that is so violent that it "breaks" the spirit of a person. The state of being a broken spirit is an injury associated with critical dimensions of existence: a sense of connection to self, others, and nature; to the vision and hopes for the future; to God and sources of meaning in life; and to the sacred, innermost core of one's soul as a human essence.

What does it mean to fracture a person's self? What constitutes a broken spirit? What does it mean when the core of the self and identity begins to fragment and unravel, like a tightly wound ball of string that gets dropped and loses its layers of thread nicely wound together? The threads end up in a pile, entangled and mixed together in ways that take time to straighten out and rewind into a coherent ball again, which never seems quite as well wrapped as it was before becoming a sprawling mass of unraveled twine.

Spirit constitutes the core, inner sanctum of the ego and the self of a person. Spirit has been referred to as soul, vital essence, life energy, and elan. Although the word spirit is not a psychiatric term, its use is universal in language. We speak of depressed and traumatized persons as having lost their "spirit." We speak of states of dispiritedness in which persons have lost that vitality and essence that characterize their identity and uniqueness. We refer to those who have suffered loss, bereavement, or profound disappointments as having lost their verve, energy, and liveliness. They are without their usual animation that others recognize through continuity and self-sameness as "them" — their unique individual quality of being.

It is important to understand the concept of a broken spirit, even if metaphorically, to successfully treat traumatized persons. Although everyone understands the meaning of a broken spirit through the experience of empathy and personal episodes of loss, failure, and trauma, it has a psychodynamic meaning of significance to how the self gets fragmented by extremely stressful events. When the self fragments, it splits into parts reflecting a loss of coherency, agency, and continuity in time and space. It is possible to speak of the dissolution of the self in many ways: dissociation, fragmentation, splitting, fracturing, disunion, rupture, disintegration, diffusion, doubling, shattering, and annihilation. To meaningfully understand how any of these relatively synonymous ways of self-alteration occur requires specification of two interrelated processes: (a) the *external* force of trauma and loss, and (b) the impact of external experience to the *internal* fabric of the ego and self-structure.

In understanding psychological trauma, it is essential to postulate intrapsychic dynamics of personality processes and how optimal states of well-being are impacted. This formulation includes appreciation for the role of allostatic transformation caused by extreme stress and internal dynamics of the self: ego-processes, defense mechanisms, and adaptive configurations in behavior and personality functioning. Allostasis refers to attempts at stability in organismic function through change following stress demands on the person (McEwen, 1998; Wilson, Friedman, & Lindy, 2001). Allostatic mechanisms involve all psychobiological systems (e.g., cognition, perception, memory, etc.). There are allostatic transformations as well to core, internal ego processes and the functions of the self (Wilson, 2003; Wilson et al., 2001). As we noted in understanding the role of allostasis in posttraumatic stress disorder (PTSD):

> Trauma impacts the psychic core of the very soul of the survivor and generates a search for meaning as to why the event had to happen. A state of dispiritedness may cause a profound questioning of existence and force belief systems to change (Wilson and Moran, 1997). The alternative of psychoformative processes may lead to a de-centering of the self, a loss of groundedness and a sense of sameness and continuity. In extreme cases, a radical discontinuity may occur in ego-identity, leaving scars to the inner agency of the psyche. Fragmentation of ego-identity has consequences for psychological stability, well-being, and psychic integration, resulting in proneness to dissociation. In many cases of PTSD, the fragmentation of ego-identity is a fracturing of the soul and spirit of the person … such a broken connection in an individual's existential sense of meaning may be a precursor to major depression, psychological surrender, and in extreme cases, suicidality and death. (Wilson et al., 2001, p. 30)

To understand posttraumatic damage following trauma, it is necessary to know the various ways that broken spirits are manifest: to learn how fragmentation, dissolution, dissociation, fracturing, and diffusion in the self, identity, and ego processes occur and reconfigure following allostatic changes within the organism. *To understand how the self is injured by trauma, it is necessary to understand optimal states of functioning and pretraumatic self-configuration.* In the fields of psychoanalysis and traumatic stress studies, many clinicians have used different terms to describe the processes of alteration in identity, consciousness, and the self-structure (see Erikson, 1968; Herman, 1992; Kalsched, 1996; Kluft, 1994; Kohut, 1971; Krystal, 1968, 1988a; Lifton, 1967, 1976, 1993; Niederland, 1964; Parson, 1988a; Putnam, 1997; Ulman & Brothers, 1988; Wilson et al., 2001). Space limitations do not permit a comprehensive review of the many contributions to our knowledge of damage to the self, especially that caused by severe trauma. However, a germane insight by Ulman and Brothers (1988) states

> It is because the self is the process, center of mental activity for organizing the meaning of experience in that a serious disturbance or interference in its ability to function constitutes a trauma. The person's sense of self or experience of the self is critical to its organizing activity. Thus, any occurrence taking an unconscious meaning that seriously challenges or undermines this sense may be experienced as a traumatic shattering of the self. ... A person ceases to secure selfhood without some center for organizing experience into meaning structures. (p. 7)

This passage helps to illuminate the critical role of the self as an organizing structure of individual experience. Broken spirits have shattered "selfs" and "fragmented ego processes," which result in states of despair, apathy, depression, "dispiritedness," loss of vitality, soulessness, and the will to thrive. The shattered self is broken into shards, which if reassembled well, can become a new architectural form of strength and beauty; a transformation of the fractured integrity of the object. However, it must be acknowledged from research on catastrophic trauma (Krystal, 1968, 1988a) that for some survivors, the self remains torn apart and incomplete. If left unglued and unassembled, it will remain broken shards with lost unity and wholeness that no longer "stick together."

THE STRUCTURE OF THE SELF AND COMPLEX FORMS OF PTSD

> The self develops through an interaction of biological maturation and a series of socialization experiences that while cross-culturally variable, still provide the evoking conditions necessary for the emergence of the sense of an autonomous, continuous, and internalized self.
>
> Froddy & Kashima, 2002, p. 10

It is a truism to say that the self is injured by trauma, especially premeditated acts of interpersonal violence and emotional abuse (Breslau, 1998; Friedman, 2000). Traumatic injury to the self is like a high-velocity bullet piercing through the body, tearing apart internal organs critical for survival. Although the severity and depth of the impact varies greatly between persons and is determined by many variables (e.g., age, resiliency, type of trauma, adequacy of support, etc.), trauma can cause wounds to the mind, soul, and body. Similarly, whereas the brain and heart are critical organs of the body, the self and ego are the core psychic organs of the mind. And, just as the brain and heart are essential structures with interrelated functions, the self and ego are dynamically interrelated in mental health, psychological growth, and well-being.

The role of the self has occupied a major focus in many of the major theories of personality and psychopathology (Monte & Sollod, 2002). Ulman and Brothers (1988) have reviewed theories and psychiatric conceptualizations of the self and the manner in which it can be damaged by trauma. The self can be shattered and result in dissociation, defensive constellations to protect narcissistic injuries and vulnerabilities, or can lead to more or less crystallized personality traits. These conclusions, of course, are consonant with many of the theories and clinical insights of Janet (1900), Freud (1919), Jung (1963), Kohut (1971), Rogers (1951), Stern (1985), Erikson (1968), Parsons (1988), Putnam (1989), Kalsched (1996), and others. Common to these clinicians and researchers is the idea that the construct of the self is central to internal organizing principles of psychological functioning. As applied to injuries to the self, without a meaningful way to understand traumatic damage to the self-structure, it is akin to trying to understand degenerative neurological disorders without understanding how the brain functions.

To fully appreciate the internal psychological injuries caused by trauma, it is useful to outline the structure and functions of the self. By understanding aspects of self-structure and its role in organizing behavior, especially posttraumatic adaptations, we can gain insight into the specific nature of the injuries and psychic scars produced by trauma.

To begin, the self is an internal psychological structure that is organized in terms of its functions and designs. Daniel Stern (1985), in his detailed studies of the development of the self in infants stated

> they seem to approach interpersonal relatedness with an organizing perspective that makes it feel as if there is now an integrated sense of themselves as distinct and coherence bodies, with control over their activities, ownership of their affectivity, a sense of continuity, and a sense of other people as distinct and separate interactants. (p. 69)

Stern's research shows that the self is an integral, organizing structural part of personality that establishes bases of self-worth (i.e., self-directed appraisals of the self as an object). As a psychological structure it provides a basis for self-esteem, a sense of well-being, and uniqueness to individual identity. The self is part of a self-object matrix in the world and establishes connections, relations, and investments of energy and value in others, whose worth is also appraised and "esteemed." The self-object matrix of significant others also serves as a component of identity formation since others recognize and confirm the individuality, existence, and importance of the individual in a larger reference group, kinship network, or community. Simply summarized, the self is a central processing unit of personality that organizes experience and adaptation (Mischel & Morf, 2003).

The architectural framework of the self-structure contains ego and personal identity processes (Erikson, 1968) that can be considered an infrastructure of the self. As defined by Erikson (1968, p. 50), identity involves a sense of self-sameness and continuity to the way in which the ego masters experience, both in time (e.g., ontological epigenetic development) and space (e.g., geographical location). The idea of identity is especially important in understanding damage to the self. Among the landmark studies of massive psychic trauma, R. J. Lifton (1967) found that among Hiroshima survivors many had lost their sense of self-sameness and continuity in time and space due to catastrophic devastation of every aspect of life, culture, and existence produced by the first atomic bomb. Lifton spoke of "vacuum" states in which the vitality of the self was emptied. Survivors of the first atomic bomb referred to themselves as "the walking dead" serving penance in "hell." Lifton observed that prolonged psychic numbing was essential for survival for many Japanese survivors. These findings, along with those from Holocaust studies (Krystal, 1968, 1988; Wilson, Harel, & Kahana, 1988a), demonstrated that both the self and ego processes could lose a sense of continuity. In *self-discontinuity*, whether radical or partial, the individual experiences a disruption, rupture, or severing of connection to self-objects and sources of psychic meaning and importance. Such survivors feel "cut off" or dramatically broken away from the threads of continuity that sustain meaning and directionality to existence. Lifton (1976, 1979) termed this radical discontinuity the "broken connection" to underscore how psychoformative modes of self-experience were altered, often permanently, by catastrophic trauma (see Lifton's [1979] discussion of connection versus separation; movement versus stasis; integration versus disintegration as subparadigms of the self).

We can speak, therefore, of a *cohesion-fragmentation continuum* as the experiential basis of the posttraumatic self. In severe trauma, the psychoformative planes of self-experience can "*invert,*" leading to a sense of *separation*, *stasis*, and *disintegration* of, or a division within, the structure. In this way, there is a "broken connection" with the past; the experiential planes of the self shift, much like what occurs in an earthquake, as internal tectonic plates shift and move under the force of gravity. If strong enough the earthquake's tremors cause fissures in the earth's surface, generating damage from the shifting internal structural plates. Similarly, in the traumatized self, the sense of worth, stability, or orderliness in daily living is lost or profoundly altered in ways associated with a sense of disequilibrium, flux, change, and alteration of what was once defined as normal living.

The psychological change that accompanies a loss of continuity and self-sameness typically involves a *loss of coherence* of the structure of the self — a crumbling of the structural components — much like that of a tall building disintegrating or imploding from explosive charges or the powerful tremors of an earthquake. As the infrastructure of the building begins to come apart, girders, trusses, and support columns pull apart, give way, break off, and, eventually, the integrity of the structure is lost — it no longer has its original architectural form or functionality. The spatial and structural configuration has changed and that which once defined the identity of the building is gone, although parts might remain that contain elements of the former structure — like pillars of the Parthenon in Athens or cross-hatched steel girders from the former World Trade Center in New York. Analogously, the structure of the self can be partially or totally injured or destroyed by trauma.

The Architecture of the Self

> The self system is an organized meaning system, guided and constructed by the organization of relationships among the person's self-relevant cognitions and affects ... the self is an organized dynamic cognitive-affective-action system and the self is an interpersonal self-construct system.
>
> Mischel & Morf, 2003, p. 32

There is an architecture to the self. It is a structure built from epigenetic life span development that has form, function, and esthetics. Although there is no consensus on the number of elements that comprise the structure of the self, we can speak meaningfully about six core dimensions: (1) coherency, (2) connection, (3) continuity, (4) energy, (5) autonomy, and (6) vitality (Leary & Tangney, 2003; Mischel & Morf, 2003; Stern, 1985). Table 6.1 summarizes and defines these dimensions. It is important to have a clear definition of the dimensions of the self and their optimal function in personality in order to understand how traumatic impacts alter their efficacy in functioning.

The impacts of trauma can alter the structural and functional dimensions of the self in many different ways. As observed by Lifton (1976, 1979) and those who have studied forms of dissociation (e.g., Chu, 1998; Goodwin & Attias, 1999; Janet, 1907; Kalsched, 1996; Kluft, 1996; Nijenhuis & van der Hart, 1999), the components of the self can undergo changes that result in a loss of functional integrity, affectivity, motivation, agency, and health. Further, within each of these dimensions, additional changes can occur to substructural components, for example, rendering changes in boundary permanence, self-other appraisals, sense of self-worth, loss of autonomy, and so forth.

In our New York City World Trade Center analogy, the twin towers lose their foundational supports after being attacked and waver unsteadily before collapsing. Steel girders, connecting rods, I-beams, soldering joints, load-bearing walls, and supportive H-welded crossbeams come apart and detach from their designed function. The cables installed to transport elevator lifts to floors of the building snap, lose their mooring, and give up their transport function. The power source is damaged causing a loss of energy to operate machinery or to provide heat, lighting, and air conditioning. Without a source of power, the building

TABLE 6.1 Core Dimensions of the Self Affected by Trauma

Dimensions of Self-Structure: Optimal Function	Traumatic Impact and Altered Function
1. Coherency: Organized Integration of Function (Functional Integrity) Self-other boundaries; locus of control in degrees in unity in experience	**Fragmentation:** Loss of integrated coherence to functional capacity. Loss of locus of control, unity, and boundary structures
2. Connection: Planes of Experience, Physical, and Psychological (Affectivity) Affective connectivity to self and others, symbolic connectivity to past and future	**Separation:** Loss of emotional ties to self, others, groups, and society. Loss of connection to self as object is psychic numbing
3. Continuity: Time, Space, Self & Others (History) Personal history, experiential flow, enduring awareness	**Discontinuity:** Loss of an ongoing sense of self in time and space. Loss of continuity with past experience
4. Energy: Drive and Trajectory of Striving (Motivation) Motives, goal-directed behavior, purposeful striving	**Immobility; Stasis:** Loss of physical and mental energy; generalized fatigue; malaise Loss of motivation and goal-directed behavior
5. Autonomy: Self-Regulation and Control Systems (Agency) Capacity for self-regulation of physical and psychological processes	**Loss of Autonomy, Self-Regulation:** A sense of self-esteem and capacity to freely self-regulate is lost or diminished. Feelings of shame, guilt, and self-recrimination are present
6. Vitality: Health and Strength of Organism (Health) The degree of optimal physical health and psychological vitality to sustain self-functions	**Illness, Loss of Vigor:** Subjective or objective decrease in health status. Experienced loss of psychic vigor. Loss of essential personal vitality can be entirely psychogenic

Source: Wilson, 2002.

becomes inert, stagnant, and nonfunctional. It cannot self-regulate when the controls of the engineering systems for power, transport, and maintenance are severely disrupted. The coherency, vitality, and energy of the structure have all been damaged or compromised, rendering its functional use severely limited, if at all.

When the bases of the self-structure and its organization are damaged by psychic trauma, the result can be different forms and degrees of self-dissolution, fragmentation, disintegration, and "implosive" self-destructiveness. Like the former World Trade Center in New York City, which initially withstood the impact of terrorist commandeered jet aircrafts, the twin towers caught fire, buckled under the immense heat, broke apart, and ultimately collapsed into a massive pile of rubble. In the end, nothing remained of the towers; they were dead and nonexistent. So, too, the self-structure can buckle, bend, break, shatter, and disintegrate in response to psychic trauma, especially that which is maliciously and malevolently designed by humankind to inflict purposeful injury to the bases of self-functioning. Torture, for example, is designed to attack the spirit, break individual will power and control it, to produce submission and surrender, and to denigrate the personhood of the victim. We have learned through traumatic stress studies that there are many psychological equivalents of torture and ways to attack the self and rape the soul (Agger & Jensen, 1993; Gerrity, Keane, & Tuma, 2000; Jaranson & Popkin, 1998; Simpson, 1993). As Table 6.1 shows, in an overly simplistic way, injury to the core self-dimensions results in a loss in the strength and functionality of self-coherency, autonomy, connection, and energy and results in malaise, illness, and discontinuity with self (i.e., the past) and others, which is so vital to a sense of kinship and community. Moreover, the "de-structuring" of the dimensions of self-structure through trauma results in disunion, fissility, or disjoining of its interrelated dimensions. Moreover, we know that depending on the age of developmental maturation in epigenesis (Erikson, 1968; Nader, 1997, 2003; Pynoos & Nader, 1993; Stern, 1985), the self-structure, personality, and the nature of adaptive ego processes will reconfigure into new structures. These new structural configurations can be understood and conceived as posttraumatic typologies of the self with attendant modalities of ego processes manifesting varying degrees of continuity and self-sameness.

Typologies of Posttraumatic Self-Configurations

A person is brought so completely to a stop by a traumatic event which shatters the foundation of his life that *he abandons all interest in the present and future and remains permanently absorbed in mental concentration upon the past.*

Freud, 1916, p. 342, emphasis added

TABLE 6.2 Trauma and Reconfiguration of the Self-Structure

Posttrauma Typology and Alterations	Ego Processes	Key Descriptors	Forms of Personality Processes and Psychopathology	Adaptational Continuum
Inert self (soul death)	Surrender	Regressed	Catanoid states: brief psychosis, PTSD	Severe pathology
Empty self	Depression	Passive	Major depression: PTSD	
Fragmneted self	Diffusion	Mistrustful	Dissociation: PTSD	Borderline disorders
Imbalanced self	Instability	Disconnected	Borderline PD: PTSD	
Overburdened self	Fixated	Overcontrolled	Obsessive-compulsive: PTSD	Anxiety disorders
Anomic self	Normlessness	Nonattached	Dysthymia, anxiety: PTSD	Adjustment disorders
Conventional self	Adjusted	Conforming	Generalized anxiety, adjustment disorder PTSD	
Grandiose self	Exhibitionistic	Insolent	Narcissistic PD: PTSD	Narcissistic disorders
Cohesive/vital self	Resilient	Flexible	Identity integration: prosocial partial PTSD	Self-esteem and identity
Psychosocial accelerated self	Postconventional	Existential	Individuation, partial PTSD	Self-individuation
Integrated transcendent self	Actualized	Unified	Self-actualization	Self-actualization

Source: Wilson, 2003.

Trauma's ability to injure the self and produce cracks in its architectural design can cause internal restructuring of its components. Table 6.2 summarizes 11 typologies of posttraumatic self-configurations. These configurations grow out of the processes of coping with traumatic impacts to personality and crystallize (temporarily or permanently) as modalities of altered structural configurations. The derivation of these typologies was based on many sources of data: (a) the clinical and psychiatric literature on narcissism and self-disorders; (b) the research on massive psychic trauma; (c) research and treatment of dissociative disorders; and (d) modern personality research on the structure of personality (Monte & Sollod, 2002). The trait constellations of the posttraumatic typologies are not to be construed as the same psychodynamic configurations of traditional personality disorders, although they can share many similarities in characteristics, symptoms, and ego-defense dynamics. The posttraumatic self-structural configurations are not necessarily pathological in nature nor should they be considered as a traditional psychiatric disorder, especially in the absence of documentable pretraumatic morbidity. The different configurations can be thought to exist on a continuum that ranges from dimensions of vacuous dispiritedness to transformative reintegration of the self in forms of actualization, individuation, and spiritual numinosity. It is possible to discern that each of the dimensions can be differentially affected, reflecting degrees of injury or impairment to the structure itself. Damage to the structure of the self results in lost functionality, which lessens its efficacy in coping with external demands of reality.

Some survivors report a loss of internal self-continuity and connection but retain a sense of autonomy, energy, vitality, and integral coherency. In extreme cases, as described lucidly by studies of Holocaust death camp survivors (Krystal, 1988a; Niederland, 1968), torture victims (Ortiz, 2001), and victims of ethnic genocide (Lindy & Lifton, 2001), the self can be destroyed, resulting in abject "psychological surrender," the cessation of striving, and the will to thrive. For such persons, posttraumatic self-configuration can be meaningfully characterized as inert, inanimate, lifeless, decimated, or annihilated. Such a profound form of alteration of the self is psychic collapsing, analogous to the demise of the World Trade Center in New York. The structure of the self unravels, dismantles, and reverts to regressive forms of primitive ego functioning at a rudimentary survival level. When the psychic core of the self dissipates structure, there might be few internal resources remaining to facilitate the construction of a new configuration, which Wilson (1980) described as a process of retrogression among severely traumatized Vietnam War veterans. The individual subjectively experiences him- or herself as "gone," "frozen," or "dead"; that whomever he or she had been before the trauma has disappeared, changed dramatically, or has been diminished in stature. What remains are fragmented pieces of the self that can be devoid of energy, hope, trust, and a viable system of meaning. Robert Lifton (1967) and Victor Frankl (1988) spoke of this posttraumatic condition as a "vacuum state" of existence — void of capacity for the creation of meaning and realizing a tangible future. In a vacuum state of emptiness, the person exists in the abyss of trauma, a kind of psychological "black hole" without end, which centripetally pulls in negative affect and experience. Such persons live with a broken spirit in the heart of darkness and despair, which I will discuss more extensively below.

TRAUMA AND RECONFIGURATIONS OF THE SELF-STRUCTURE: A CONTINUUM OF FRAGMENTATION TO INTEGRATION

We can conceptualize posttraumatic reconfiguration of the self as typologies of personality profiles. Table 6.2 illustrates 11 typologies of self-reconfiguration following extreme trauma and key descriptions of ego processes, personality, and psychopathology associated with each form of posttraumatic structural reorganization. Table 6.2 orders or classifies the typologies from the most fragmented and damaged to the highest level of transformation, reintegration, and optimal functioning. The typologies can be considered to be arranged on a continuum from pathology to health; from broken spirits to transcendent ones; from loss of humanness to self-individuation, and the capacity for the numinous connection to the existential meaning of life.

Based on the clinical literature on trauma and its impact to personality functioning (Goodwin & Attias, 1999; van der Kolk, McFarlane, & Weisaath, 1996; Williams & Somer, 2002; Wilson, 1980), we can define and identify the types of reconfigurations to the self following an extremely stressful life experience. Space limitations do not allow a full description of each posttraumatic typology summarized in Table 6.2. However, a capsule summary will be provided and further elaborated in Figure 6.3, which analyzes how optimal functioning is breached by trauma. The typological classification can be understood as reflecting the dimension of motives, affect, self-organization, and ego functioning.

The Transfigurations of Personality

> Trauma and transfiguration of the self are sculpted by fate, God, and the propitiousness of the historical moment.
>
> John P. Wilson, 2003

Inert Self

The *inert-self* typology consists of traits characteristic of the most severely damaged person. Trauma's impact to the self has broken his or her spirit and the will to thrive (Krystal, 1988a). The motivational striving has ceased, even for safety, and he or she appears to manifest extreme helplessness, evidence of surrender, and the will to survive at the most basic level. In previous studies (e.g., Krystal, 1968), they have been labeled as the "walking dead," the slave state of mind, or other terms indicating psychological stasis (Niederland, 1968). Their affective states are flat and nonexpressive — inert, lifeless, empty, vacuous, and numb. The personality processes and forms of psychopathology include catanoid states, brief psychosis, paranoid states, and PTSD. The inert self has regressed into a state of extreme helplessness and slid passively into autistic withdrawal, which Krystal (1988a) described as the catanoid state. Key words are surrender and regressed.

Empty Self

The *empty-self* typology consists of traits of passivity, depressiveness, and an exhausted sense of being depleted of energy (Wolfe, 1990). They experience malaise, loss of interest in activities and relationships, and are isolated from others. They withdraw into themselves in self-absorbed ways, unable to actively initiate social relations. They manifest what Lifton (1976), Frankl (1984), and others have referred to as "vacuum states." They are insecure, dependent, safety-seeking; desiring structure, order, predictability, and guidance from others. They lack joy and a capacity for positive affect. They maintain strong traits of oral pessimism, doubt, and loss of trust in the world (Erikson, 1952). They might have prevalent suicidal fantasies and ideation. Their personality processes and forms of psychopathology include major depression, dependency, schizoid states, and PTSD. Key words are depressive and passive.

Fragmented Self

The *fragmented-self* typology consists of traits of identity diffusion, fragility, and strong feelings of discontinuity within themselves and with others. They experience themselves as "unglued," "not whole," and as "falling apart." They are chronically anxious and vacillate in attachments with strong emotional intensity. Erik Erikson (1968) described these processes as identity diffusion. Their ego processes are diffuse and inconsistent in the adequacy of self-care and efficacious in psychosocial functioning in work and affiliative relationships. Under stress, they are especially prone to dissociation, as was typically experienced peritraumatically during trauma (Marmar, Weiss, & Metzler, 1997). Their personality processes and forms of psychopathology include dissociative disorders, dependent personality characteristics, and PTSD. Key words are diffusion and mistrustful.

Imbalanced Self

The *imbalanced-self* typology consists of extreme emotional instability. They fear abandonment and being left alone without others to rely on for nurturance, reassurance, love, and security. Ernest Wolfe (1990) described such persons as craving "external mirroring" from stable self-objects. They have a loss of internal coherency caused by trauma, which expresses itself in severely disrupted interpersonal relationships. They are emotionally labile, prone to outbursts of anger or states of anxiety and agitation, when they perceive a loss of connection of themselves, even temporarily, with others. Unlike the inert self and empty self, they mobilize disrupted affects to manipulate others to enhance self-mirroring. Their personality processes and forms of psychopathology include manipulativeness, instability, borderline personality disorder, PTSD, and transient depressive episodes. Key words are instability and disconnected.

Overburdened Self

The *overburdened self* is fixated to the trauma experience and overdefended with characterologically rigid traits. They use obsessive and compulsive behavior, rituals, and a rigid pattern of living to cope with a fundamentally pervasive anxiety, which reflects fears that to "let go" will result in decompensation or agitated, overwhelming anxiety states (Shapiro, 1981). They typically have high energy levels that are employed to fortify and rigidify the self-components of coherency, connection, and continuity. They "ward off" the impact of trauma to their sense of vitality through denial, reversal, and compensatory overactivity in work and efforts to maintain routine, discipline, and unswerving patterns of daily living. Horowitz (1976/1986, 1999) observed that such persons "jam" attention by frenetic work to block traumatic memories. Their personality processes and forms of psychopathology include obsessive-compulsive disorders, adjustment disorders, characterological rigidity, and PTSD. Key words are fixated and overcontrolled.

Anomic Self

The *anomic self* is adrift and rootless in society. Trauma's impact has led them to detach and isolate in self-contained, alienated ways from others. They experience normlessness, which reflects the lack of internal coherency and connection within the component self-factors. They are mistrusting of others and autonomously self-regulated by maintaining a controlled distance from conventional social norms, which they scorn, reject, or criticize. Their ego processes are lacking in resiliency and strength, which is compensated for by maintaining normlessness, which serves defensively to quell episodes of dysthymia and anxiety. The anomic self is characterized as a loner, whose experience of trauma has caused the individual to be wary and suspicious of intimate involvement or commitments of self that would require investments of his or her unsure sense of self-coherence and capacity for genuine connection to self and others. Frankl (1984) described such persons as existentially empty in meaning systems of belief. Their personality processes and forms of psychopathology include depressive episodes, anxiety states, and PTSD. Key words are normlessness and nonattached.

Conventional Self

The *conventional self* is adjusted to society following trauma. They seek safety and affiliation with others to reassure normality to life (Wilson, 1980). The conventional self is able to maintain autonomy and vitality and to actively seek to enhance feelings of coherency and efficacy with others in affiliative, approval-seeking ways that reassure a meaningful sense of connection within themselves. They are overly conformist and group oriented. They adhere to in-group values and norms. They seek approval for adherence for upholding values and behaviors that bring adulation of esteem from others who serve as reference points of traditional conventionality (Wilson, 1980). Their personality processes and forms of psychopathology include generalized anxiety disorder and PTSD. Key words are adjusted and conforming.

Grandiose Self

The *grandiose self* represents a posttraumatic adaptive personality style in which the striving for recognition prevails. The striving for recognition from others is motivation for the attainment of depleted, injured, or lost self-esteem. The grandiose self has high levels of energy and autonomy, which fuel behaviors to achieve external acclaim, praise, and admiration from others who are viewed as important and powerful icons of genuine success. Paradoxically, the grandiose self lacks true self-cohesion and continuity in identity. In the wake of trauma, their narcissistic injuries are aggravated, leading to various defensive attempts to protect their denied inner vulnerabilities. Erwin Parson (1988a) described war veterans with such psychological injuries as angry at the loss of appreciation for their suffering and in turn became demanding and manifest a sense of entitlement to special treatment. Their personality processes and forms of psychopathology include the spectrum of narcissistic disorders, depressive episodes, and PTSD. Key words are exhibitionistic and indolent.

Cohesive Self

The *cohesive self* reflects resilience in ego processes following trauma. Such individuals "spring back" from extreme stress and adversity; they regain their "shape" and functionality. The cohesive self has an internal locus of control, vitality, and security. Their identity reflects integration and continuity. Kahana, Harel, and Kahana (1988) described such persons as resilient, hardy copers. They are prosocial in moral values and orientation to society. They evidence postconventional adaptation, reflecting concerns with universal justice, fairness, ethics, and truth. Key words are resilient and flexible.

Accelerated Self

The *accelerated self* is an autonomous, individualistic outsider in society. They are existential iconoclasts. They are highly individuated and autonomous and live without synchronicity in social norms. They are resolute, resilient, morally principled, altruistic, and self-directed. They manifest self-individuation as a result of overcoming trauma. Their self-structure is coherent, associated with positive affect and generativity (Erikson, 1968). However, as a consequence of trauma, they have a discontinuity with the past, their former selves, and a connectedness to others. Their self-metamorphosis is a shape-shifting, creative protean transformation of their inner resources, talents, and human personality propensities. The accelerated self reflects a "speeding up" in epigenetic ego development as a result of trauma (Wilson, 1980). The emergence of normative age-related crises appear prematurely in personality. They are psychosocially accelerated or "fast-forwarded" ahead, dealing with critical life-stage issues in an advanced way before their usual or customary time in life-span development. They manifest creative patterns of coping. Wilson (1980) described such persons as "having transformed traumatic impact into prosocial humanitarian modes of functioning." Key words are existential and individuation.

Integrated Transcendent Self

The *integrated transcendent self* is characterized by structural integrity. The components of the self reflect optimal functioning in self-actualizing modalities. Frankl (1994), Lifton (1976, 1979, 1993), and Jung (1950) described such persons as transcendent in their overcoming personal trauma. The integrated transcendent self has successfully overcome adversity, extreme stress, and trauma in an optimal way. Their self-structure is configurationally integrated. It has transcended the pretraumatic self; evolving beyond self-individuation to the ability to function optimally in self-actualizing ways. Such persons seek growth and challenges that enrich the sense of vitality and autonomy of existence. Their personality processes include spiritual transcendence, the unity of self in the world with wisdom, and a capacity to have peak experiences of the numinous. The integrated transcendent self is the apotheosis of spiritual transformation of personality into a unity of oneness (Jung, 1950). Stated differently, they have transformed trauma into an evolved self of actualized organismic potential. Key words are unified and self-actualizing.

Summary

The typologies represent a continuum of posttraumatic adaptational forms of personality processes that range from severe pathology (e.g., inert self) to optimal mental health (e.g., self actualization).

SELF-DISSOLUTION AFTER PSYCHIC TRAUMA

> Transformations of personality are by no means rare occasions … the alteration of personality in the sense of diminution is furnished by what human is known in primitive psychology as "loss of soul."
>
> Jung, 1950, p. 53, par. 213

In an optimal structural configuration, the self is a unified whole and can be visualized graphically as a mandala, circle of unity, or as various symbols of wholeness. Figure 6.1 presents a graphic representation of *primary forms* of self-dissolution following severe trauma: (a) the inert self, (b) the empty self, (c) the anomic self, (d) the fragmented self, (e) the overburdened self, and (f) the imbalanced self. The figure represents the fractures in the unity of the self. The key descriptors that characterize the respective ego processes include surrender, depression, normlessness, diffusion, fixation, and instability. The figure shows a simplified way of visualizing how the self can fragment into new posttraumatic configurations. The wholeness of the self-configuration is impacted by trauma, splintering into segregated parts. These descriptive characterizations are quite similar to forms of narcissistic injury to the self-described by Heinz Kohut (1977) and Ernest Wolfe (1990). Narcissistic injury, or damage to self-esteem and the functional integrity of the self, can be considered universal in posttraumatic self-reconfigurations, a fact observed by Freud (1920a) in his last major theoretical analysis of traumatic neurosis presented in *Beyond the Pleasure Principle* and in earlier writings: *On Narcissism* (1911) and *Anxiety, Inhibition and Symptoms* (1914). More recently, Parsons (1988a) presented a model of how trauma leads to posttraumatic self-disorders, adapted from Kohut's work on forms of self-psychopathology, especially among severely traumatized Vietnam War veterans. Clinically, psychodynamic self-object relations theory and ego psychology are congruent with the depiction illustrated in Figure 6.1.

POSTTRAUMATIC ALTERATIONS IN THE SELF: THE LOSS OF STRUCTURAL INTEGRATION, COHESION, AND FRAGMENTATION

The various forms of self-dissolution produced by trauma can readily be understood as a loss of structural cohesion. As such they represent changes in adaptation from optimal states of functioning. Trauma's

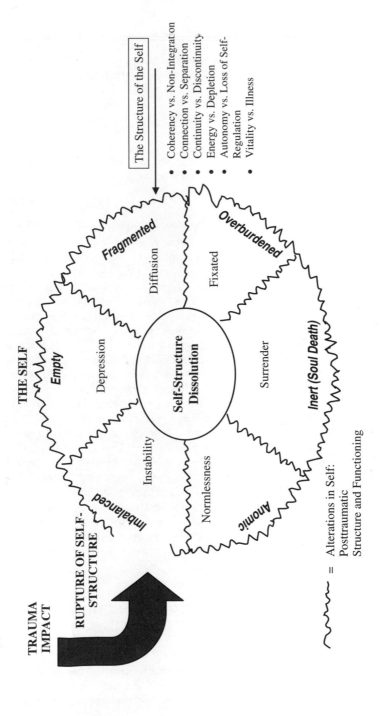

Fig. 6.1 Primary Forms of Self-Dissolution After Psychic Trauma (Source: Wilson, 2002)